Wood to Water

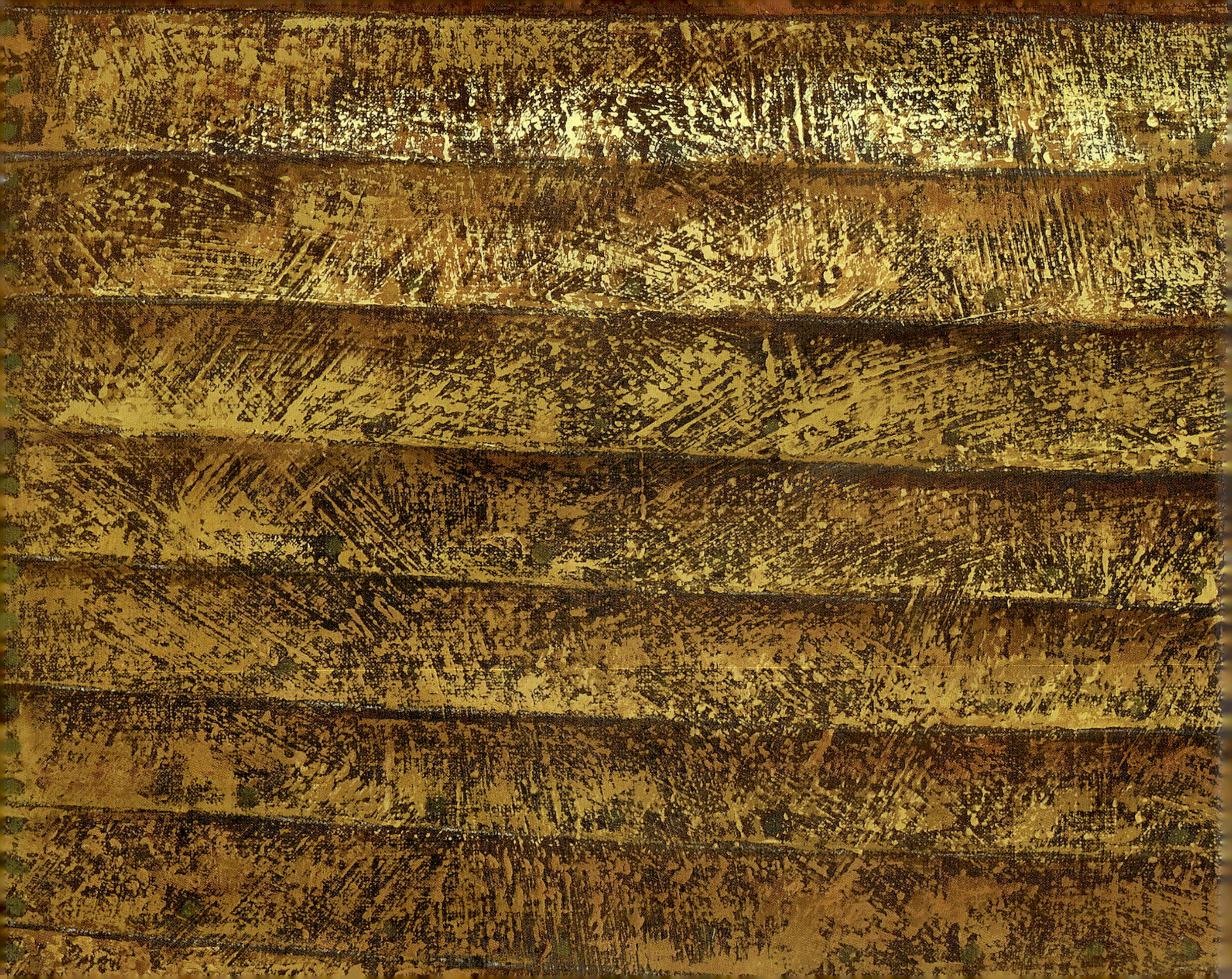

Wood to Water

JAMES DODDS
National Maritime Museum Cornwall

Jardine Press
2019

This book accompanies the exhibition
Wood to Water, James Dodds, National
Maritime Museum Cornwall October 2019
following on from a major exhibition of the
same title in 2015 at Firstsite Colchester
focusing on the boats of the East Coast.

NATIONAL
MARITIME
MUSEUM
CORNWALL

Jardine Press Ltd 2019
ISBN 978-0-9934779-6-6

Publication design by Catherine Dodds

nmmc.co.uk
jamesdodds.co.uk
jardinepress.co.uk
workingsail.co.uk
messums.com

supported by

Sir John Fisher Foundation

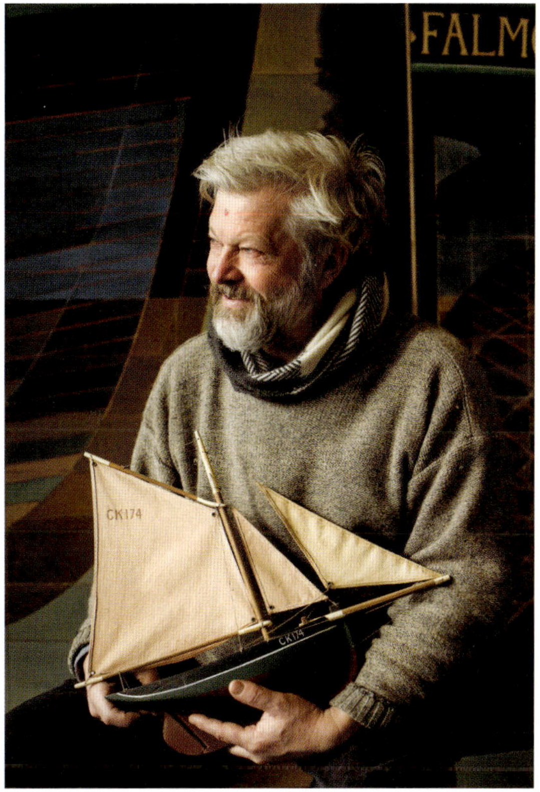

Boats have evolved over centuries to suit the sea conditions and materials available to build them. Boats are shaped by the sea. 'Wood to Water' is a travelling exhibition inspired by the vernacular boats of the British Isles. This show focuses on Cornwall and the working boats of Falmouth. I'm very happy to be showing my linocuts and paintings in this wonderful building again, in a museum that celebrates and is dedicated to small boats, vessels that float, fly and fire the imagination. As an artist and former shipwright it has been invigorating to draw on the museum's collections and the very rich maritime heritage of Cornwall.

I would like to dedicate this exhibition to all who keep the boatbuilding and seamanship skills and traditions alive.

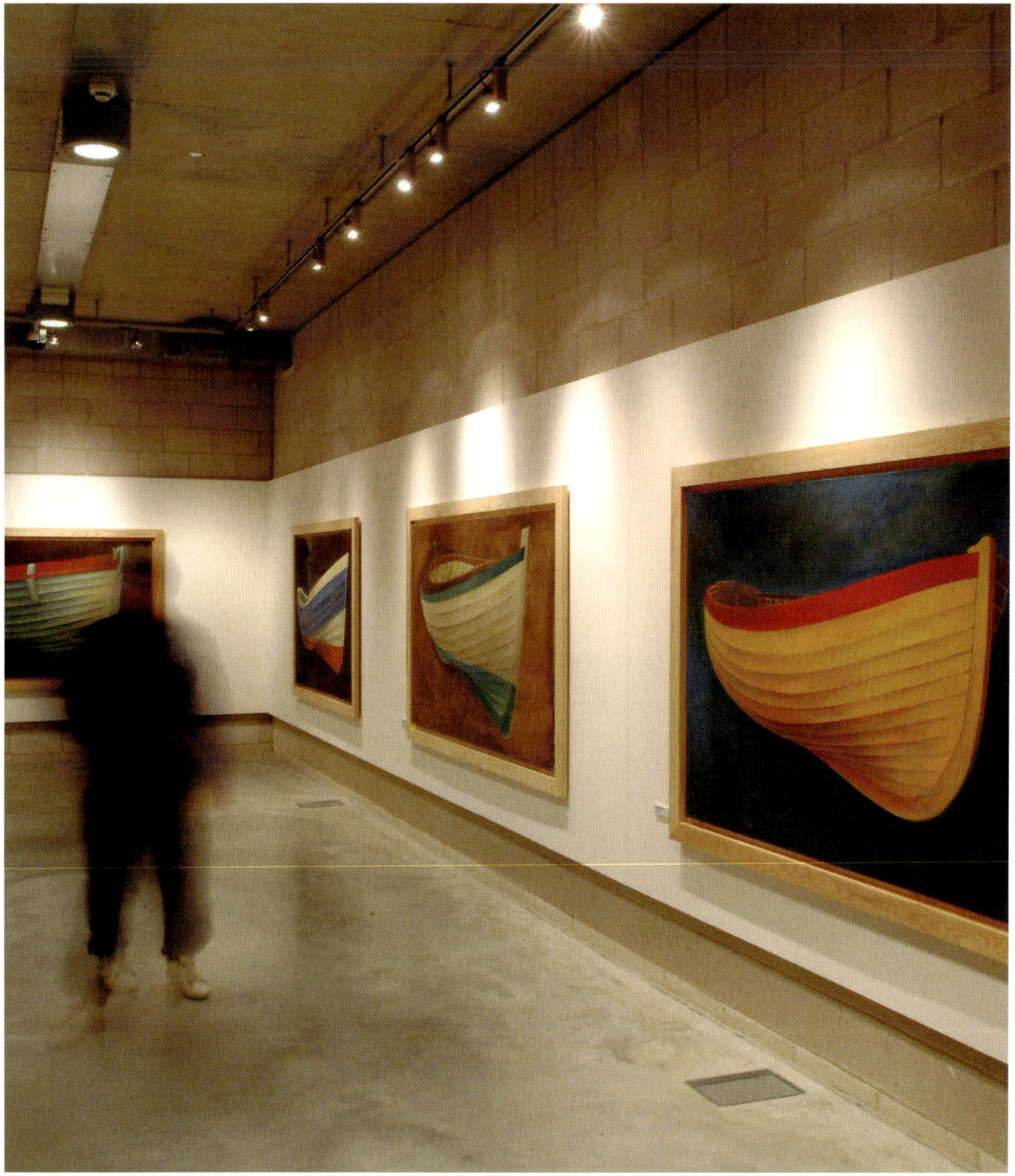

Foreword

It is a great pleasure to welcome James Dodds back to the National Maritime Museum Cornwall. This is our second collaboration – when the Museum opened its doors to the public in 2002, James was the very first artist to exhibit his work here and it was our very first temporary exhibition.

This is a natural venue in which to display James's work. His subject is small boats and we have by far the largest collection of boats in the UK. Among the 152 boats in our stewardship, is *Curlew*, one of the few remaining Falmouth Quay Punts, and we are particularly thrilled that James has chosen to include her amongst this new body of work, as well as a Falmouth pilot cutter, the largest painting James has ever undertaken.

In his introduction to *The Harbours of England*, the art critic John Ruskin, the bicentennial of whose birth is being celebrated this year, confessed that there was just one thing that he still regarded with 'unmitigated amazement', the one object he could never pass without the renewed wonder of childhood:

The blunt head of a common, bluff, undecked sea-boat, lying aside in its furrow of beach sand. The sum of Navigation is in that. You may magnify it or decorate as you will: you do not add to the wonder of it. Lengthen it into a hatchet-like edge of iron,—strengthen it with complex tracery of ribs of oak,—carve it and gild it till a column of light moves beneath it on the sea,—you have made no more of it than it was at first. That rude simplicity of bent plank, that can breast its way through the death that is in the deep sea, has in it the soul of shipping. Beyond this, we may have more work, more men, more money; we cannot have more miracle.

This is what James's art captures: the workmanship and unpretentious beauty of the traditional British wooden boat: no museum could be more delighted to host this exhibition than us.

Richard Doughty
Museum Director
National Maritime Museum Cornwall
June 2019

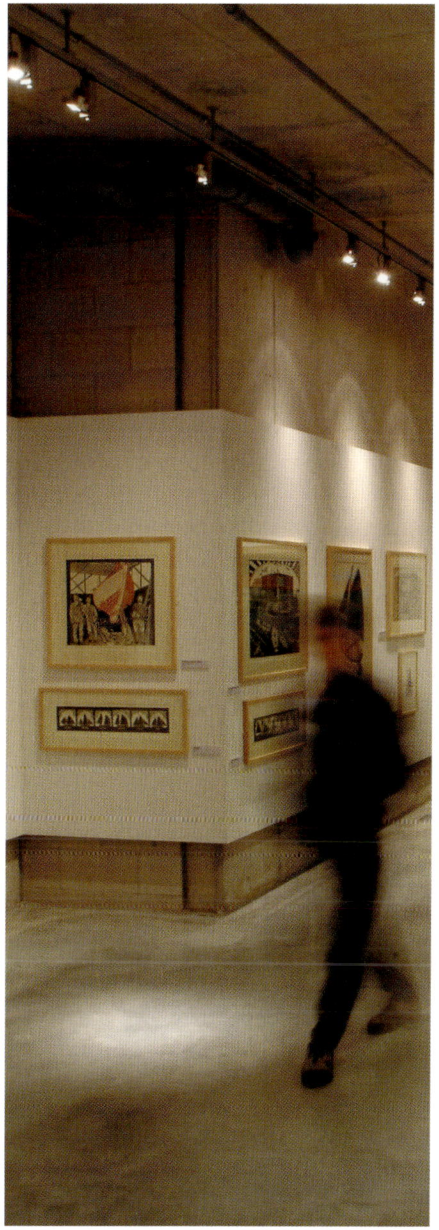

Esther Freud

Novelist

I became intrigued by James Dodds some years ago when I first read *Tide Lines*, the book about his life and work by fellow east coast citizen, Ian Collins, the two of them born 'in an elemental region that has far more sky and water than earth.' I was a judge of the New Angles prize, in the middle of writing my own Suffolk novel, immersed in the poems, stories, and images of East Anglia, but this was the book that touched me most. The quiet drama of Dodds' life, the romance of it, the search for a story that he needed to tell, the satisfying culmination of finding it. In the years since, I have often leafed through its pages, admiring the detail of the lino prints, the beauty of the Essex landscapes, and above all, the paintings of the boats. The boats are Dodds' masterpieces – his models – each one as different as a human sitter. Glossy, dilapidated, sturdy, elegant, we see them whole, aged, clothed, in disarray, stripped to their skeletal construction. He shows us the insides of them, the colours, chosen, and those that have evolved. He shows us what he sees, and makes it possible for us to see it.

Now I find myself standing in his Wivenhoe studio. It is minutes from the house he shares with his wife Catherine and their two grown children, on the site of an abandoned ship yard. He tells me that where we are standing now is the exact spot where for centuries great ships were built, sailing out along the river Colne, and off around the world. The walls are hung with paintings for a new show. All boats, oil on linen, apart from one self portrait, and a series of small heads.

It's thirty years since he last painted a portrait – and he found, when he returned to boats, he was looking at things differently. The colours were altered, his technique had changed.

These pictures, all made in the last seven months, ripple with vitality. They are luminous, restless, as if they might dart away to sea, and I find myself glancing towards the door where there is an actual boat that he and Catherine sometimes row along the river to find a place to have their lunch.

James Dodds tells me about the inspiration for each painting. A Friendship Sloop was found in Maine at the time of his last American show, another in Truro near to where his son is studying art – a faithful recreation of the 1852 Pilot Cutter, *Vincent*. There is an Essex Oyster smack that was rebuilt last year, and the Colchester smack, *Shamrock* he sailed as a boy. He likes to paint small, working boats, examine the way they have evolved, how they have been affected by sea conditions, adapted, improved upon. He is obsessed with their structure. He thinks of a Stubbs painting, a horse, suspended – Stubbs, apparently took apart a horse to see how it was made. But Dodds doesn't need to take apart a boat, because he's seen their insides, fitted them together, sailed and repaired them. He knows their history, can see the Viking influence of a boat from the Shetlands, the stout build and smooth hull of one from Hastings, how its shape is suited to the short seas of the English channel. He appreciates how the sharp, fine clinker hulls of the traditional East Coast are suited to the long Atlantic swells.

It seems inevitable that James Dodds should find his forte painting pictures of boats, but that was not always the case. For a long time he was searching around for the story he wanted to tell, big stories, world stories, and then in 2000 he was offered a solo show at a gallery in Colchester, and unable to decide what to produce, he was advised by his old friend and fellow artist, Helen Napper: Paint a boat.

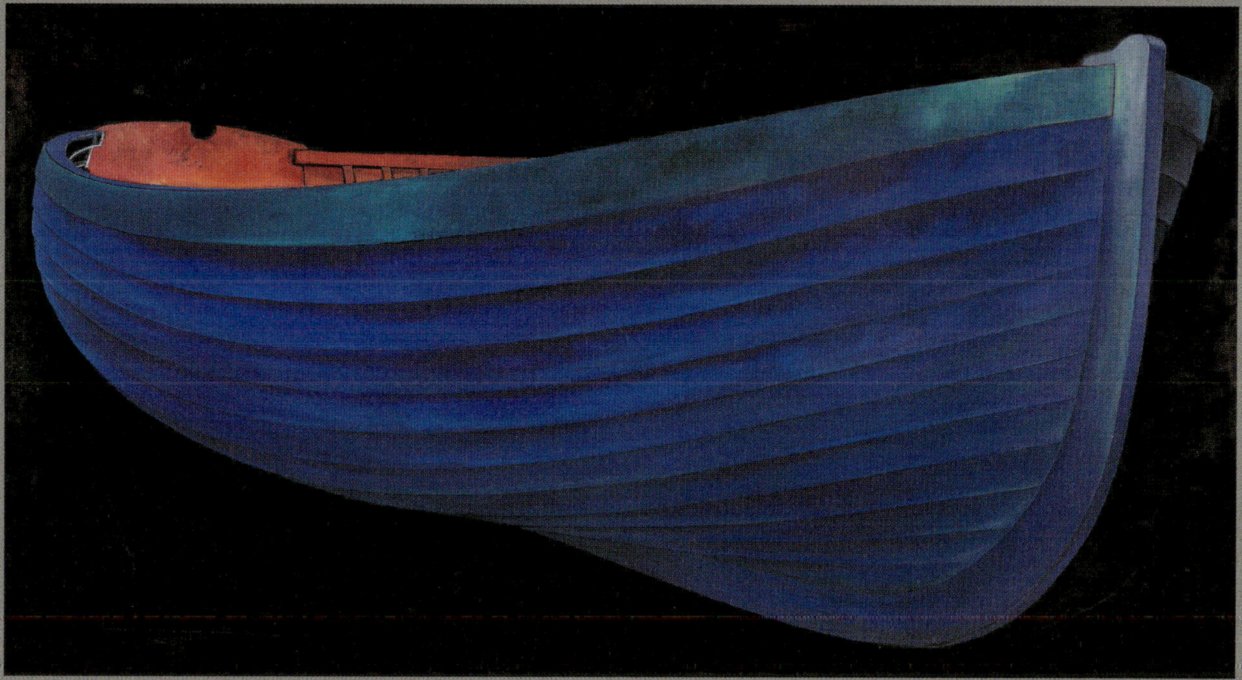

Blue Boat
(Oil on linen. 2000. 122 x 244cm)

'Whether we are sailing people or not we are all aware of the enormous symbolic, even mythical connotations of the boat, from the ship of fools to the voyage of life, from the burning of boats to the carrier of hopes. Floating in front of its dark background, the Blue Boat, small as a boat yet monumental as an image, is open to all sorts of readings… It permeates the whole of James' oeuvre to date and a theme that every viewer must pursue according to his or her own experience and imagination…

Looking at it now, without sailors in it or waves around it, I cannot think of a more impressive and convincing example of a shipwright actually building a boat without leaving the painter's studio.'

Thomas Puttfarken 2000

He hesitated. A boat was too simple. Too easy. Who would want to buy it? But all the same he began. And there it was – *The Blue Boat* – a gleaming suspended miracle of craft and art, the red slither of its interior, a glimpse of safety.

The sea has always been a large part of James Dodds' life. He grew up in the coastal town of Brightlingsea, learned to sail early, found himself a weekend job as a trainee mate on a Baltic trader aged fourteen, sailing out of West Mersea and depending on the wind direction up and down the coast to explore a river course from North to South. During school holidays he sailed across to France and Holland, and when school was finished, with one O'level in art which he took early, he was apprenticed to a boat builder in Maldon for which he received £8 a week.

'With that first boat, it felt as if I was building it on the canvas. The two sides of me, the builder and the artist, one focused on art and colour, the other on practicalities. The artist was waiting to see how it would evolve, the builder was telling me – I had his voice in my head: *There are twelve planks…*' He laughs. 'If I can stop thinking, the hard thing about painting is that it's easy.'

Outside his studio there is a commemorative plaque to the old shipyard. There is a lino print detailing how it used to be. He points out to me where each building once stood and how he has adapted it, including the parts he liked best, and as we talk his, square workman's hand trails fondly over the inscription: Cooks Shipyard Site. Reproduced by kind permission of local artist James Dodds. He nods towards his house to show how very local he is, and I think of a story in *Tide Lines*, of how, as a boy he was overhead telling a stranger that his father, the illustrator Andrew Dodds, was in fact a shipwright. He wanted his father to be like other fathers, he wanted him to be part of the community, so he could be too.

There are three working fishing boats docked against the quay of the old yard. The *Lily Grace*. The *Twilight Star*. 'That one,' he points to the *Lady K*, 'has been cockling alone the Colne. They've claimed squatters rights,' he grins. 'That's good.' And we walk back across the newly developed dock, past the one remaining boat builders shed, towards his home.

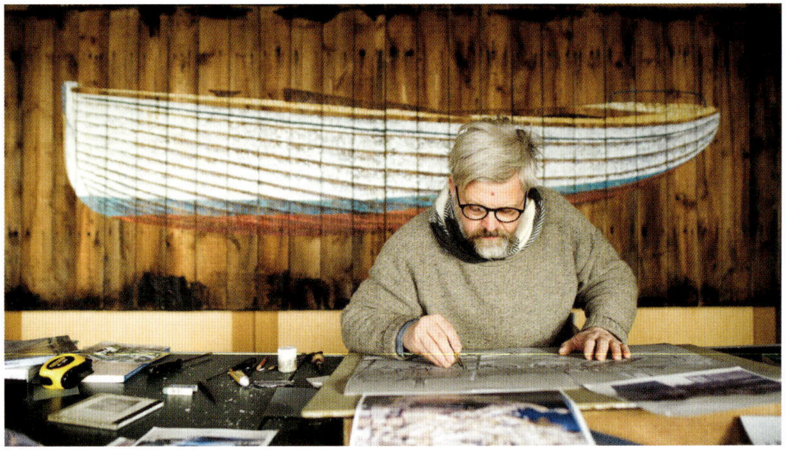

(Right) ***Fowey River Class Dinghy***
(Oil on linen. 2018. 90 x 120cm)
Built by Marcus Lewis.

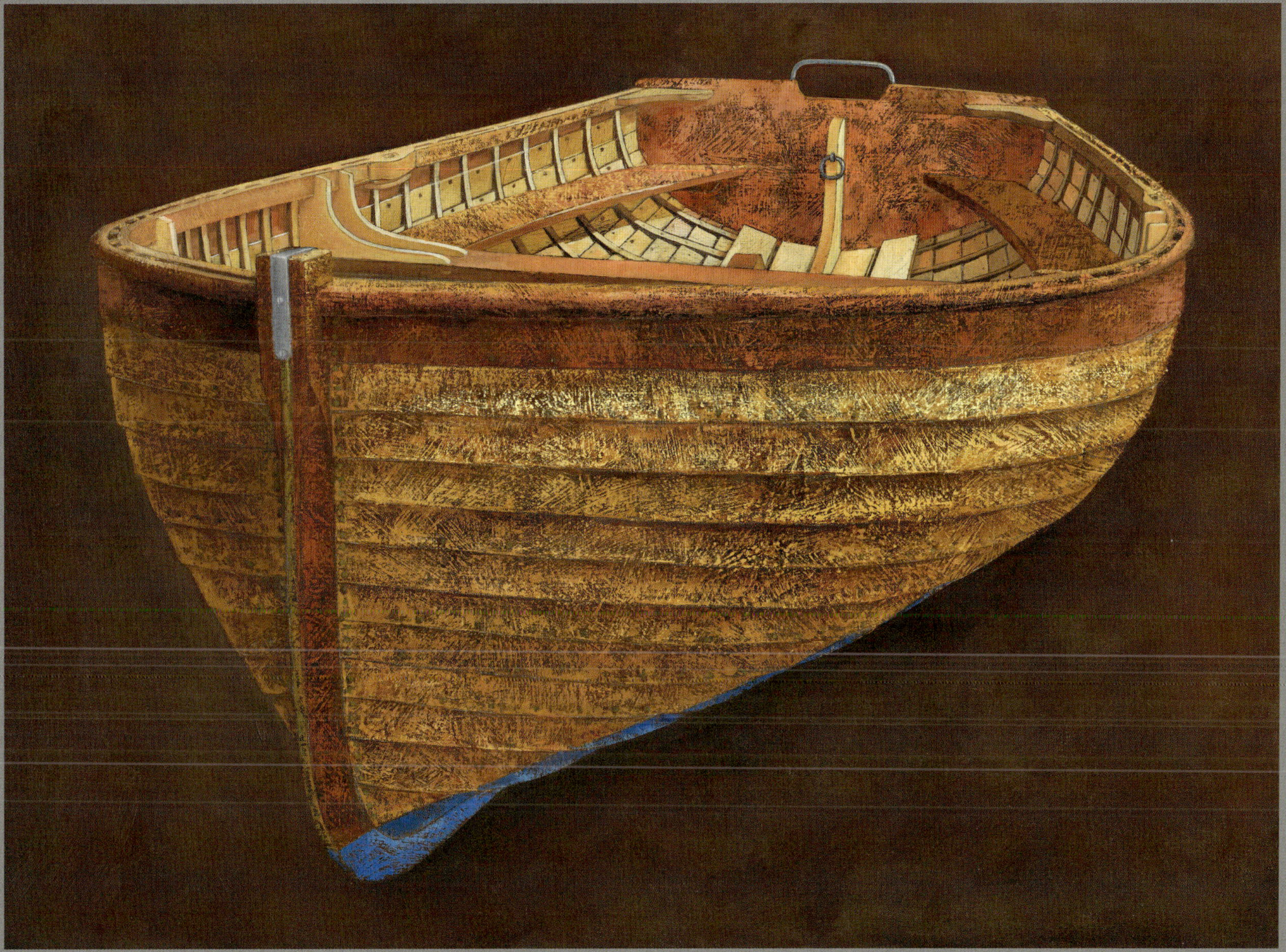

PILOT CUTTERS

Luke Powell
workingsail.co.uk

The Power of the Wind

Cornwall has always held a very close relationship with the sea; the land is stony windswept and difficult to work. So its people have always turned to the sea for their livelihood. Fishing and trading have carried these people far and wide. This narrow land jutting out into the western oceans is Britons gateway to the world, all maritime trade passes its shores. Since ancient times, ships crossed oceans from the far off Mediterranean Sea, seeking Cornish Tin to feed the Bronze Age. As times moved on, new worlds were discovered and the Cornish were amongst the first to build ships of venture, bringing Inca gold to Elizabeth and her realm. Cornish sailing ships carried the raw produce from the empire to feed the furnaces of industry. Through these endeavors a thriving industry of wooden shipbuilding grew and survived almost into modern time.

The Cutters Legacy

Ships sailing in across the oceans, heading towards the rocky coasts of Cornwall, with only rudimentary navigation to give a rough idea of their position. Seeking a safe haven, they eagerly sought local knowledge. Cornish folk would put to sea in all weathers, in their brave little cutters, heading west searching out incoming ships, and so placing a man aboard, at a good fee, to guide them in. The harder the winds blew, the faster the ships were driven towards the rocks, and the more these pilots were needed. Over the centuries their cutters grew to perfection, developed to survive and flourish in some of the wildest conditions in the world.

Built for Speed and Strength

These men developed their profession to a high standard. With a good cutter they could earn well, but if they were slow, there were no wages, only the strong survived. This created a most beautiful vessel fit for purpose, fast to compete with the other cutters and yet seaworthy to survive the harsh conditions. Sailing west beyond the isles of Scilly in search of ships, carrying eight pilots they would keep going, only returning once all were placed. At times if another sail was sighted the skipper of the cutter would also ship off as a pilot, leaving only the boy to sail this large vessel home.

People of the Sea

Although Cornwall developed a large maritime commerce, this was very rural and pre-industrial. Ships and cutters were financed by the community, the 64 share system allowed anyone to invest even small amounts, from the butcher to the candlestick maker, many shares were held by the women of the community. These ships were built out on the open beaches of the village and sailed by the men of the village, and victualled by the village. This bought the profit back into the community, creating a wealth that could not be gained from the land. And in turn this was reinvested in shipping. The more impoverished the land the greater the incentive to invest in the sea.

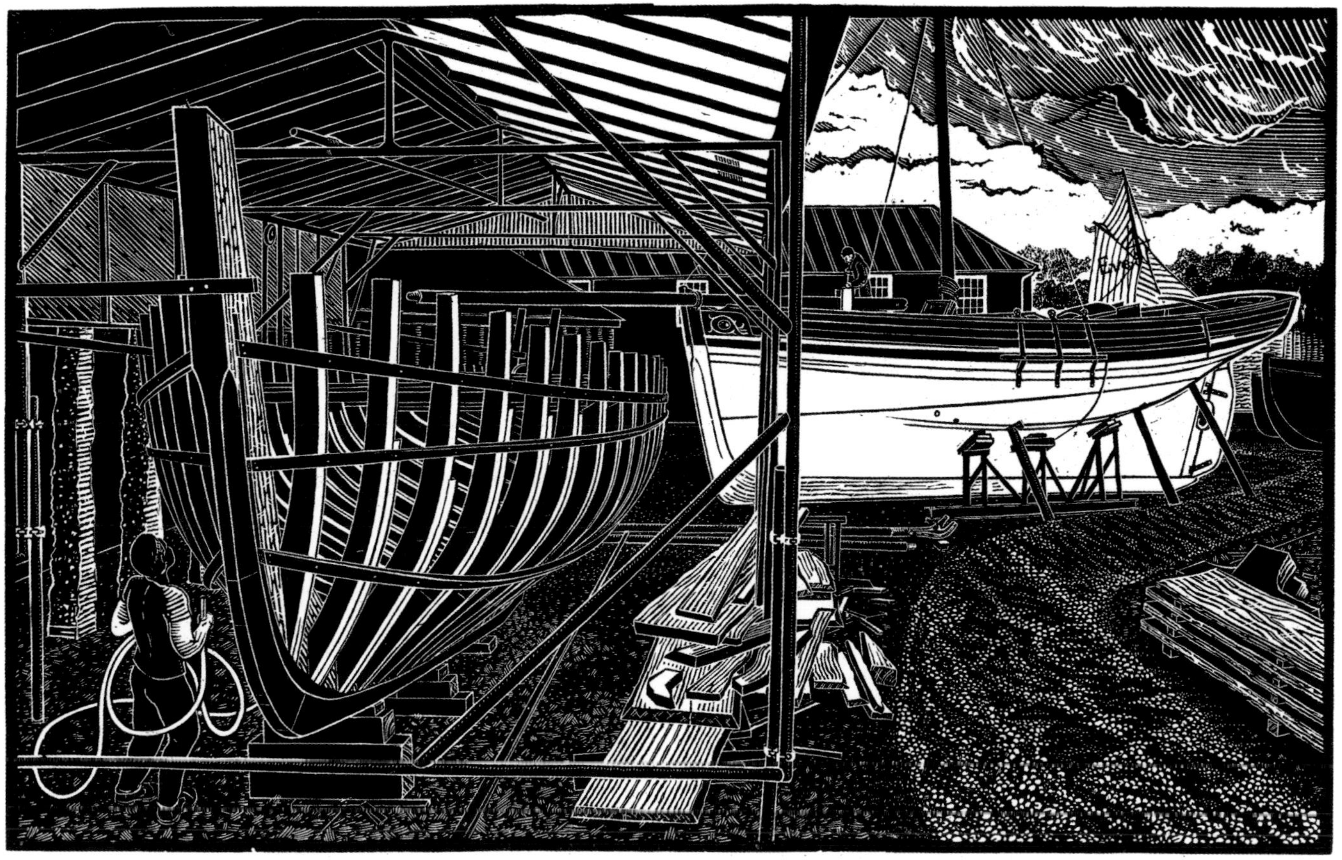

New Pilot Cutters, Gweek
(Linocut. 2004. 44 x 68cm)

This linocut shows Luke Powell's fourth pilot cutter *Hesper* in frame with *Agnes* standing finished behind.

Although we did not meet in our early lives Luke Powell and myself learnt the shipwright's trade within a few years of each other in and around the Thames estuary, rebuilding the iconic Thames sailing barges and converting them back to sail and motor barges. At this time they were just finishing their cargo carrying days. From that point on our careers took different courses. He has perfected his skills building many new pilot cutters, a vessel arguably at the peak of its sailing evolution. As for myself I like to think I am celebrating the skills learnt in my youth with people like Luke. Working boats have evolved over the centuries to fit the needs and conditions of the seas they worked. You could say boats have been shaped by the sea but in truth it has been made by the faith, skill and ingenuity of centuries of boatbuilders.

A Cornish Hero

Edward Pellew was son of a Cornish packet captain who died when Edward was young, leaving the family impoverished. Edward ran away to sea, aged fourteen, from Truro Grammar School. Through great daring and ability in the American War of Independence, he rose through the ranks in a time when merit was rewarded. In the Napoleonic Wars he became the greatest frigate captain of all time. Based at Flushing, across the waters from Falmouth he would sail out to attack the French and had many daring battles with enemy frigates, capturing and bring them home as prizes. He showed immense humanity to both his crew and the enemy, becoming great friends with the French captains he fought.

A Great Ship Reborn

For many years there has been a great desire to resurrect a legendry Falmouth Pilot Cutter, and rekindle wooden shipbuilding in Cornwall, teaching a new generation the art of the shipwright, before these skills are lost forever. We chose to call our new vessel the *Pellew* in honour of this great Cornish hero. We chose to faithfully build one of the longest lasting and best documented of the cutters, the *Vincent*, a vessel originally built in 1852 for the Vincent family of St. Mawes. She worked successfully for 70 years until being retired in 1922, ending her days as a houseboat at Freshwater on the Percuil River.

Building a New Legend

Through the kind support of the Truro harbour we have set up the Rhoda Mary Shipyard on the bank of a river where so many fine wooden sailing ships were born. In this yard we are recreating a traditional environment where we hope many projects of historic importance will take place. The yard is named after a famous schooner that we hope one-day to rebuild here. We plan to nurture and train young people in the art of shipbuilding, and create a new generation. Once launched the *Pellew* will remain based in Truro and sail the seas giving opportunities of apprenticeships in the traditional trades and seamanship associated with such a vessel.

Towards the Future

This project is set up as a Non-for-profit Community interest Project, and has been greatly supported by many people from the local community and further afield.

These are early days, but we hope to grow and take on a constant flow of young people, training them in the art of traditional boatbuilding and then sending them out into the world to secure a future for themselves. As we progress, we will reach out to a network of local businesses seeking sponsorship for our apprentices and in turn these businesses will benefit from the skill leval that will come out of this project.

New Falmouth Pilot Cutter, Pellew
(Linocut. 2018. 42 x 70cm)

This was the stage the *Pellew* was at when I first visited the new Rhoda Mary shipyard, Truro. It shows the frames and the first of the planking going on. She is 68 feet and entirely built of oak. This is the first of the buildings and planned slipway that will make up the exciting new shipyard project led by Brian Pain. The *Agnes* is tucked in behind her. Luke bought the *Agnes* back from her American owner and sailed her across the Atlantic. She is now a charter vessel run by Jo Powell of Working Sail.

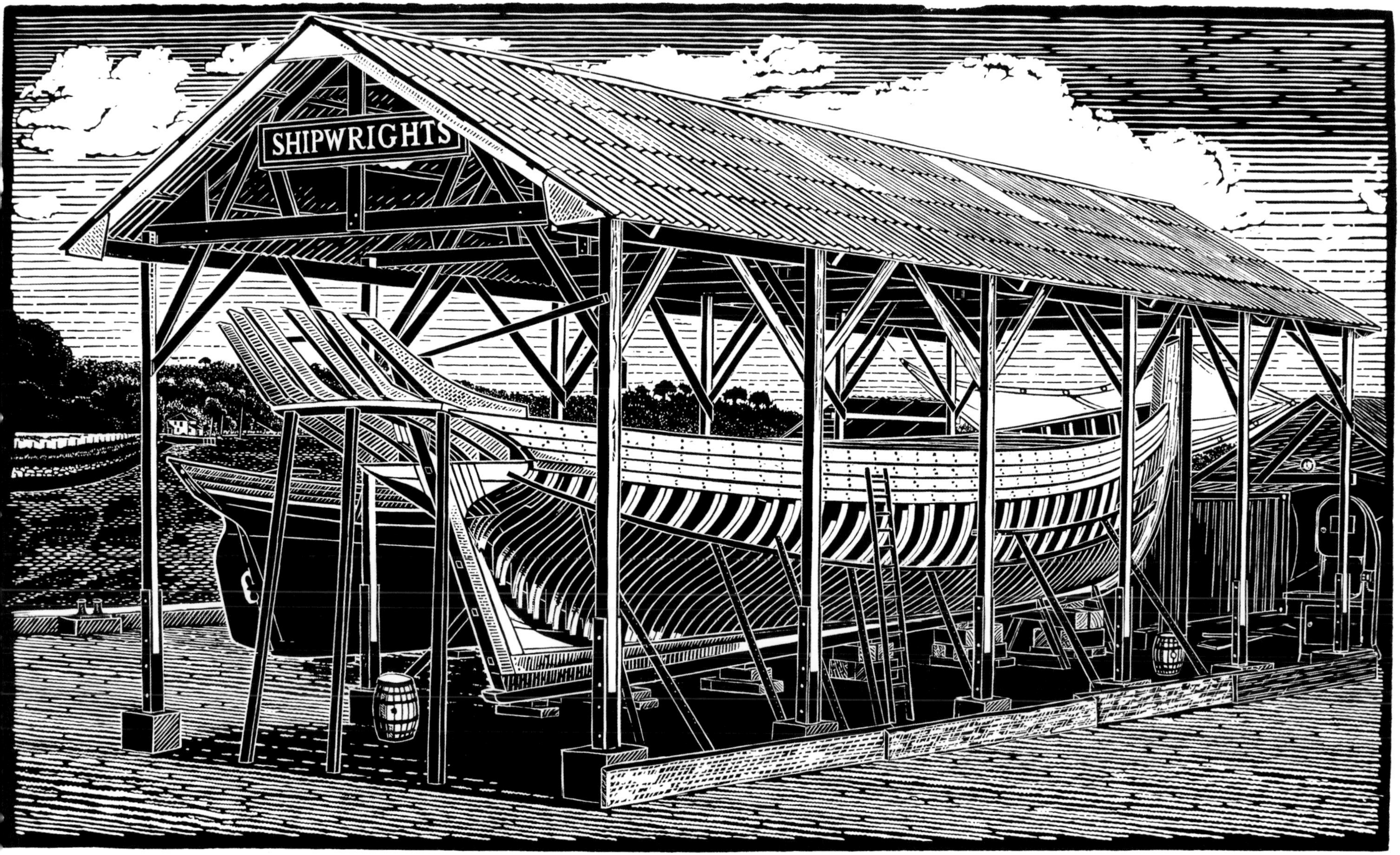
SHIPWRIGHTS

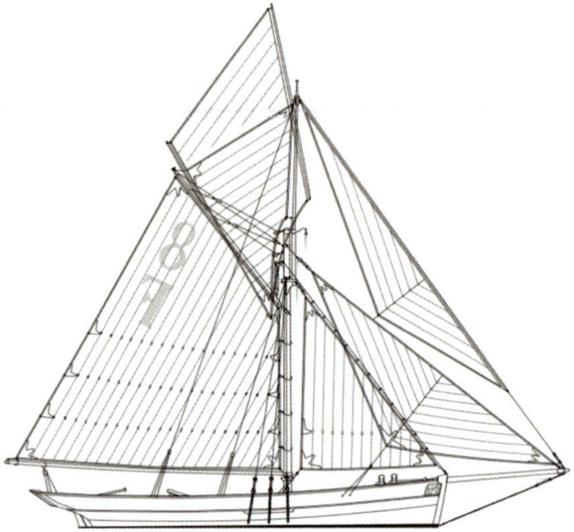

Sail plan and profile of *Pellew* drawn up from a half model of *Vincent* by Luke Powell.

Vincent towards the end of her life with a cut down rig.

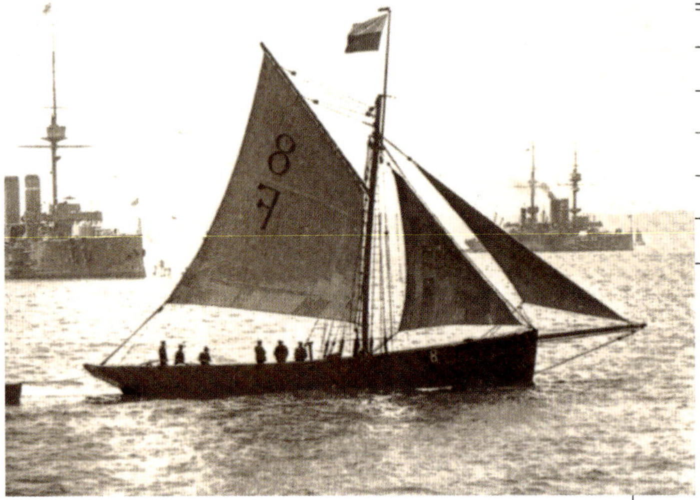

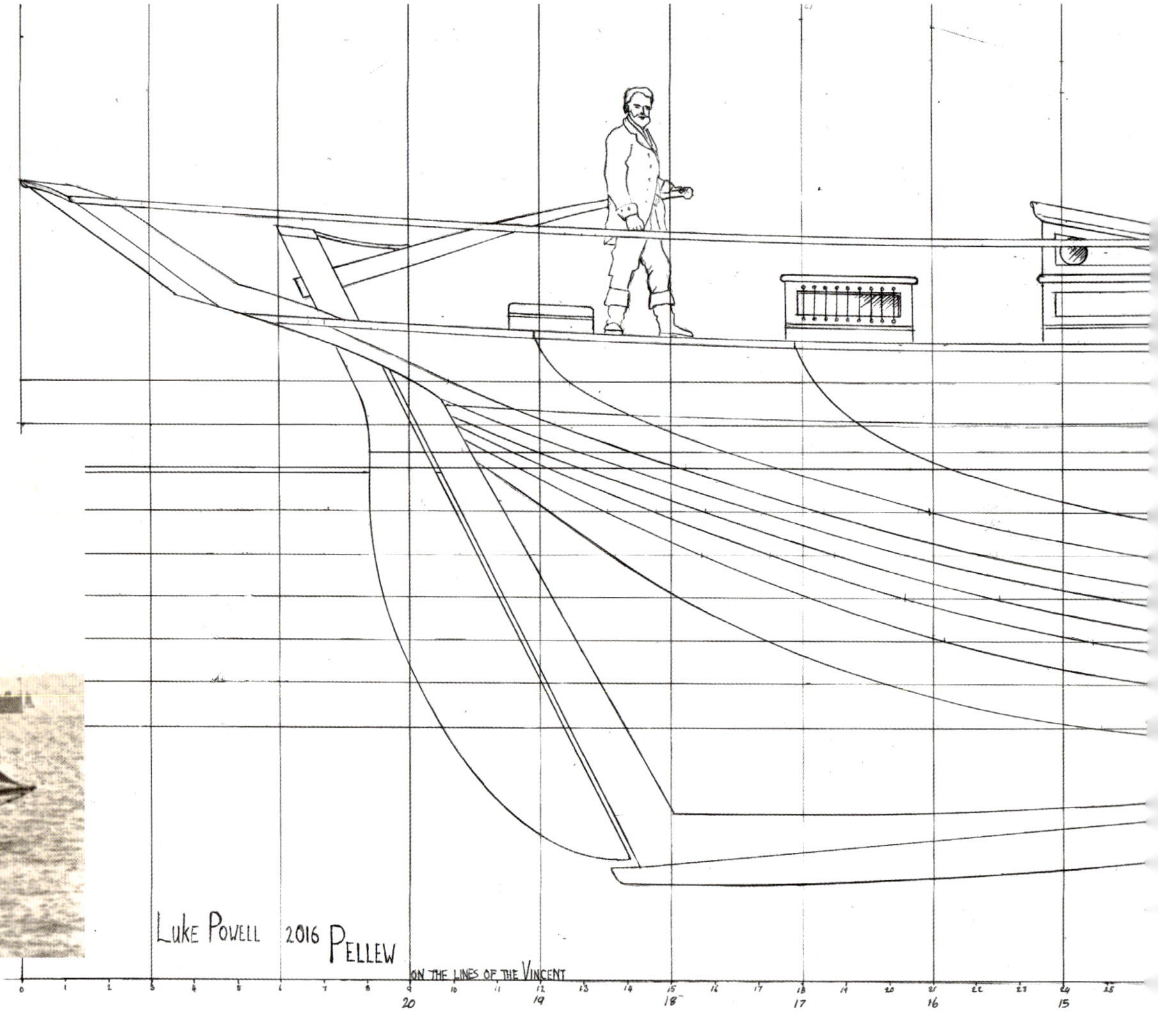

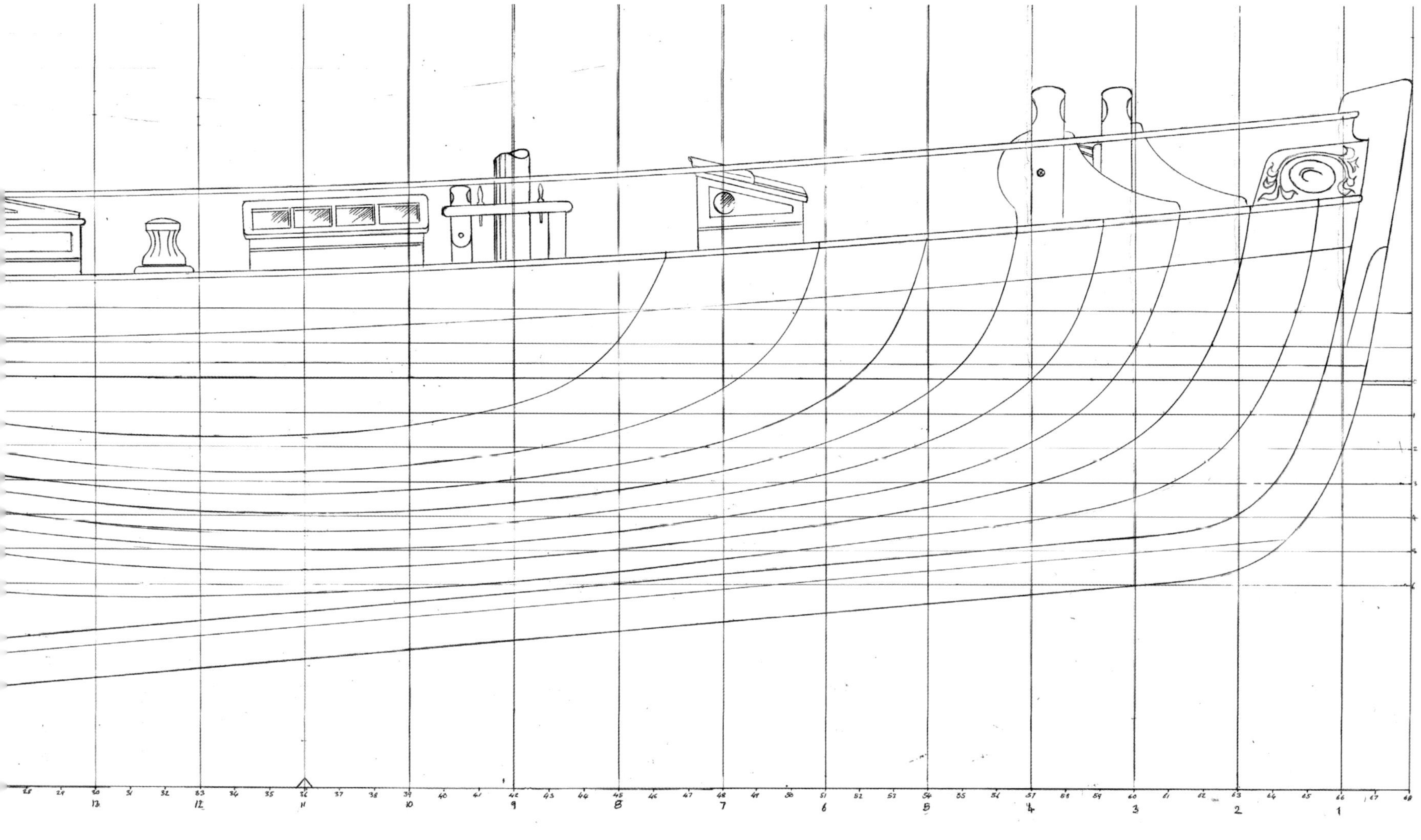
13
12
11
10
9
8
7
6
5
4
3
2
1

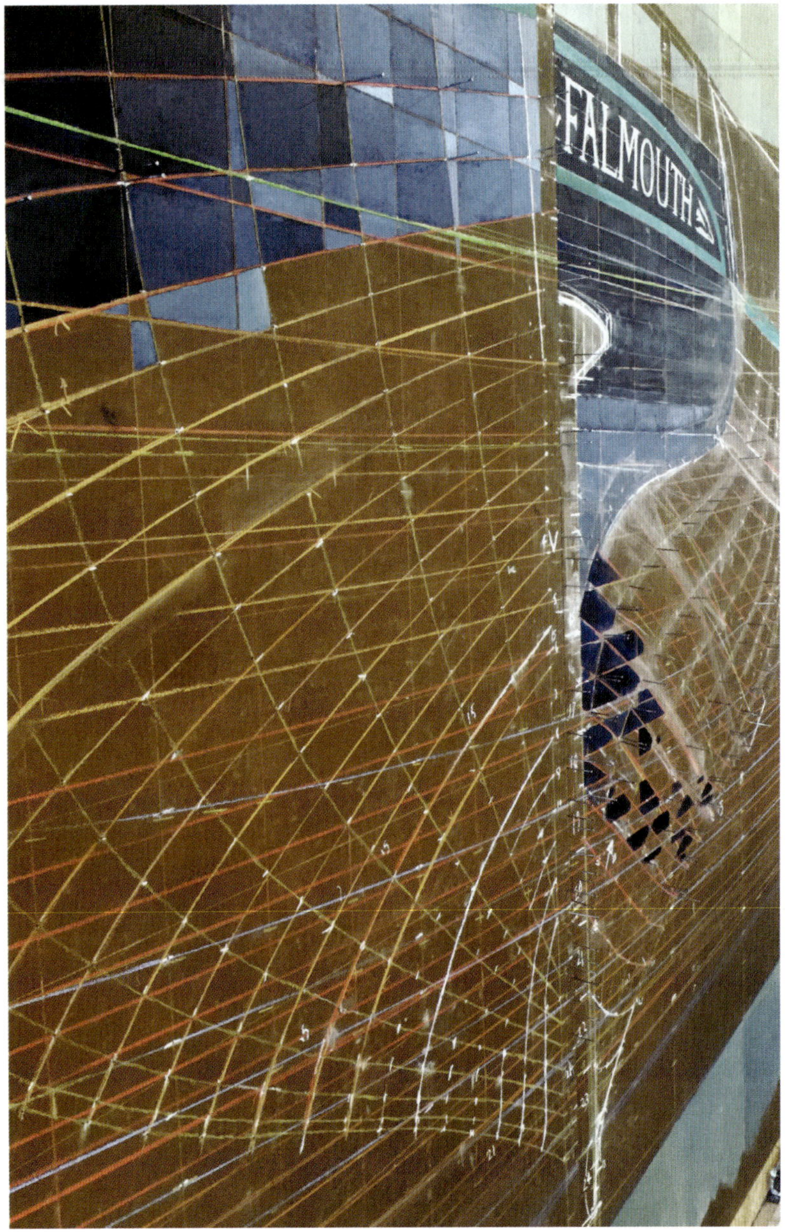

The White Line

When cutting a linocut or drawing out a painting I am working with a white line on a dark background in much the same way as the loftsman works with chalk on a dark mould floor. When lofting out the paintings I am working in coloured pencils to differentiate between the station, buttock and waterlines.

The mould loft was a loft area with a large flat floor, often with limited standing headroom. This was where a boat, to be built from a naval architect's drawing or builder's half model, was drawn out full-size on the floor. Sometimes the floorboards were laid diagonally so they did not get confused with the lines of the drawing.

It was a hallowed sort of place where you had to take your shoes off and stoop under the low parts of the eves. The loftsman had the air of a wise man, the fount of all knowledge, which of course he was as far as the boat was concerned. In fact, the loftsman was usually the foreman in a small yard.

The mould loft floor would be prepared with a black gesso, and a grid drawn with a straight edge and chalk lines. The curved lines were made by driving in nails and bending long straight wooden battens onto them. The proof that the drawing was right was if the curved lines were fair. This sometimes meant correcting the architect's small scale drawings. When the drawing was completed to the loftsman's satisfaction he would make moulds (templates) for the main structure of the boat with all the bevels marked that the curved timber had to be cut to.

The lofted paintings are on plywood board so that I can drive nails to bend battens round and I've found it easier to do this on the wall rather than on the floor. It also helps to be able to see the whole thing when I start painting. As any boat builder would know there is room for error when scaling up from a small drawing: these inconsistencies get ironed out when bending a batten and I've adopted much the same approach when working from original drawings.

(left) Lofting out the Pellew from Luke Powell's drawings onto six plywood boards. My painting is one third scale of the new 68ft pilot cutter.

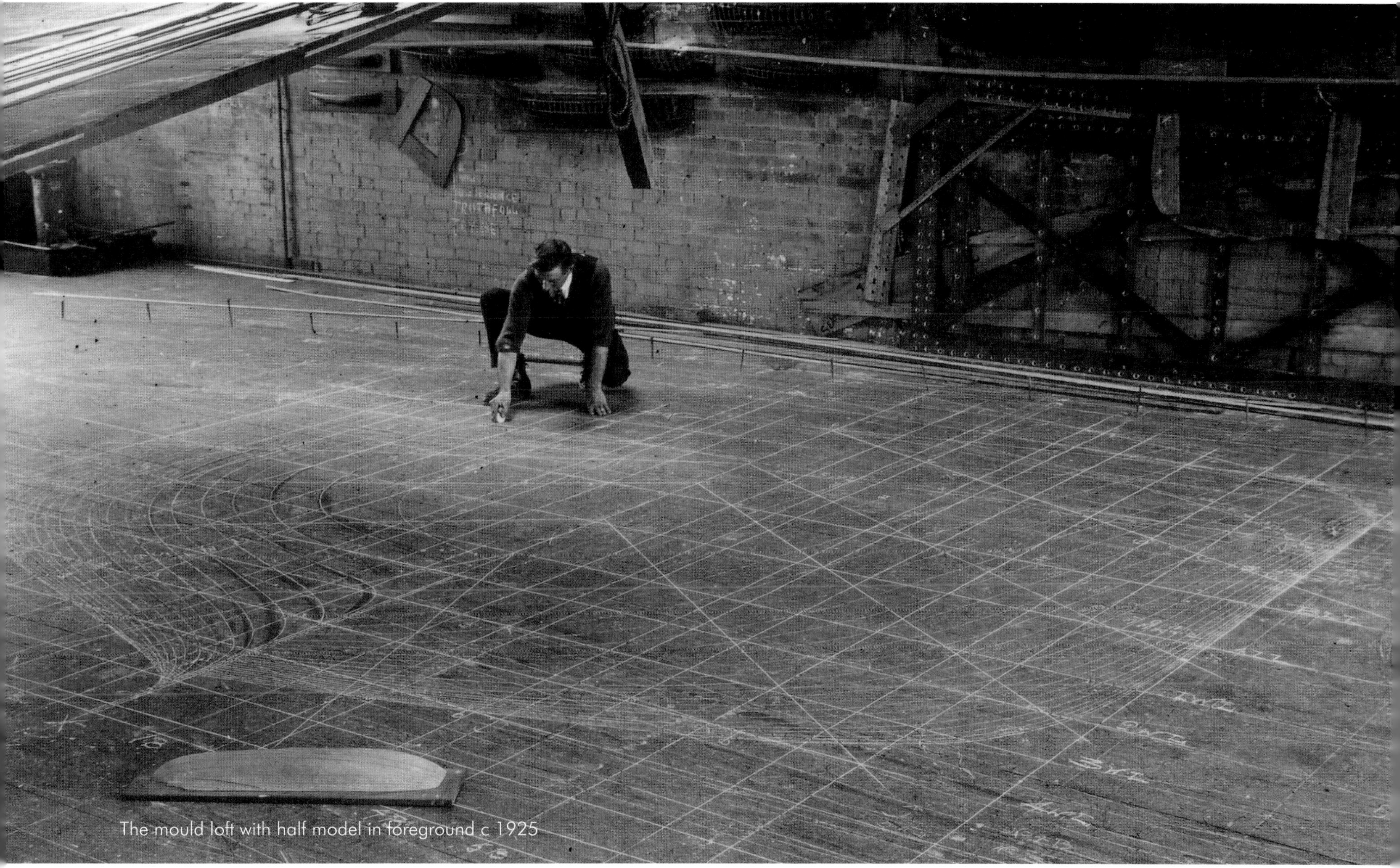

The mould loft with half model in foreground c 1925

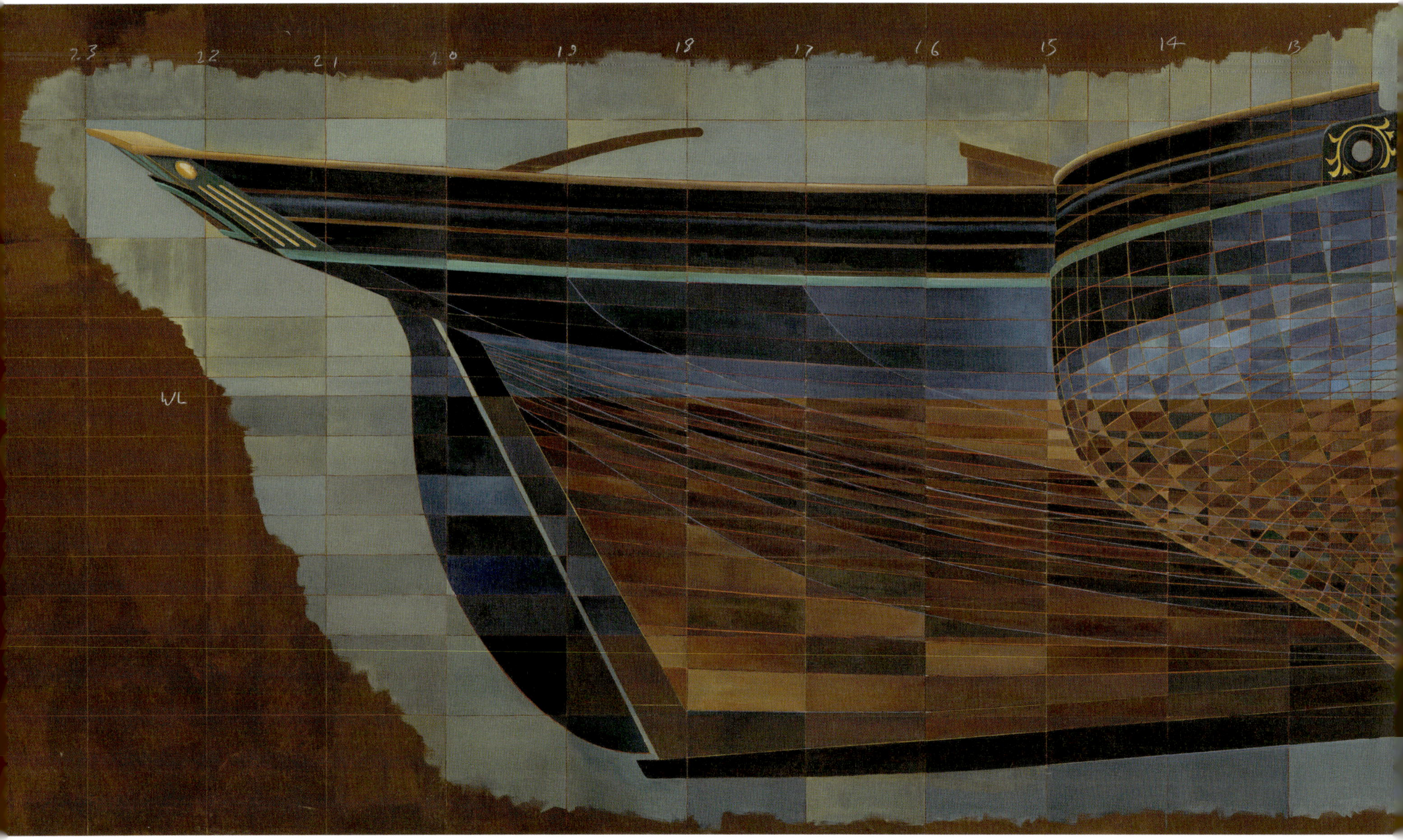

Falmouth Pilot Cutter, Pellew (Oil on 6 gesso boards. 2018. 214 x 732cm)

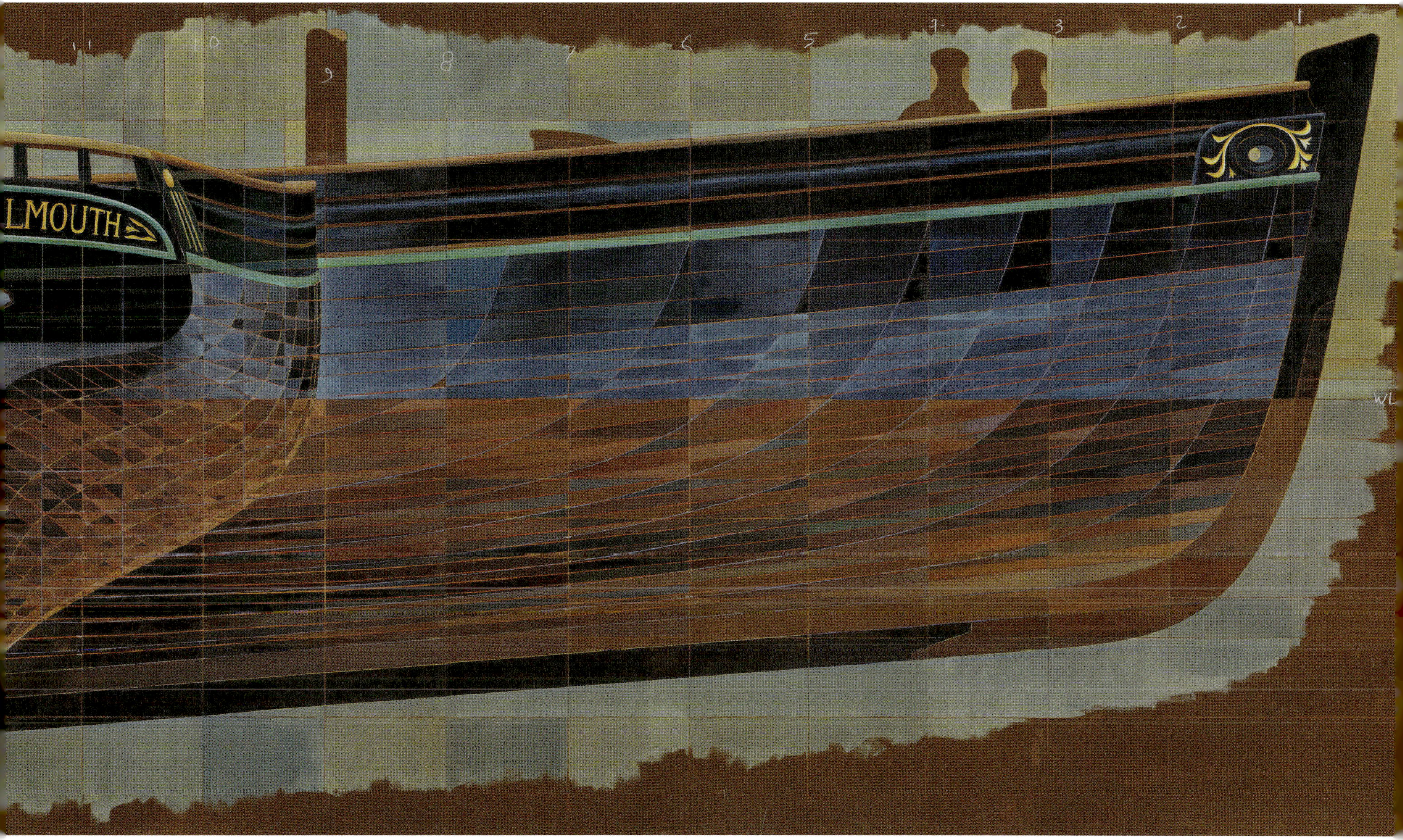
LMOUTH
WL

TRADITIONAL BOATS OF FALMOUTH

Tony Pawlyn
Researcher

Falmouth Packets

For 150 years, from 1689 to 1851, the Falmouth Packets, swift sailing craft of modest dimensions, were the principal craft connecting the British Isles with their allies in Portugal, and their colonies in the West Indies, and on the North American continent; and later into the Mediterranean, and South America. Relatively small vessels – most less than 25 metres in length, they carried government dispatches and correspondence; instructions to commanders overseas; commercial correspondence, and international intelligence, as well as diplomatic and mercantile passengers. These modest packet-boats were a fundamental element in the international intelligence and commerce of the nation across the western world.

Servicing all the needs of these packets, a host of support trades grew up in and around the harbour. Key service industries that carried the commercial welfare of the port and its inhabitants into the future after the cessation of the packet service in 1851.

Falmouth for Orders

One of the spin-offs of the packet service was the establishment of a relatively fast overland mail service between Falmouth and London – about three days for letters to travel in either direction in the1700s, which reduced to two days in the early 1800s. Thus it came about that masters of ships returning from distant climes, lacking current information on the state of the markets for their cargoes (which might be anywhere from Glasgow, Liverpool and other Irish Sea ports, and Bristol Channel in the west; or around the British Isles to the east, for North Sea ports, and even ports in continental Europe), found it essential seek the advice of the owners of the cargo for their orders as to a port of discharge. Falmouth's good inland communications, westerly location, and secure anchorage, made it ideal for this purpose. This practice was widely adopted, and the phrase "for Falmouth for Orders," was frequently endorsed on the 'Bills of Lading,' for their cargo. Within a week or ten days captains would have their answers, and while they were waiting, their ships could make good the ravages of the voyage prior to sailing for their final port of discharge.

This practice of sailing "Falmouth for Orders," continued until the creation of worldwide telegraphic networks in the 1860s and 70s, enabled some masters to be given advance notice of ports of discharge, which reduced the demand, and it was finally eliminated by the general adoption of ship-to-shore radio communications after the First World War.

Arising from the number of vessels calling at Falmouth, three classes of sailing boats, and a number of rowing boats were adopted to service the needs of visiting vessels.

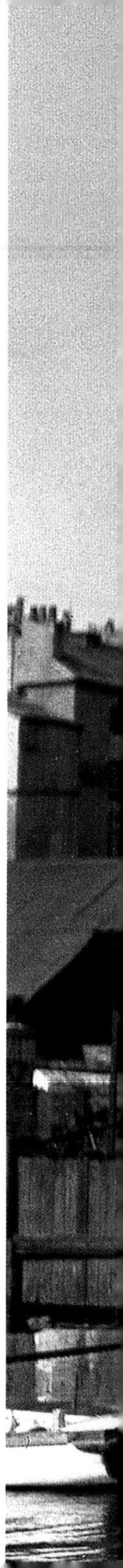

Three-masted schooner *Donald & Doris* of Bideford alongside Harris's wharf in Falmouth Harbour, at the back of High Street. Greenbank Laundry building in the background. 1934.

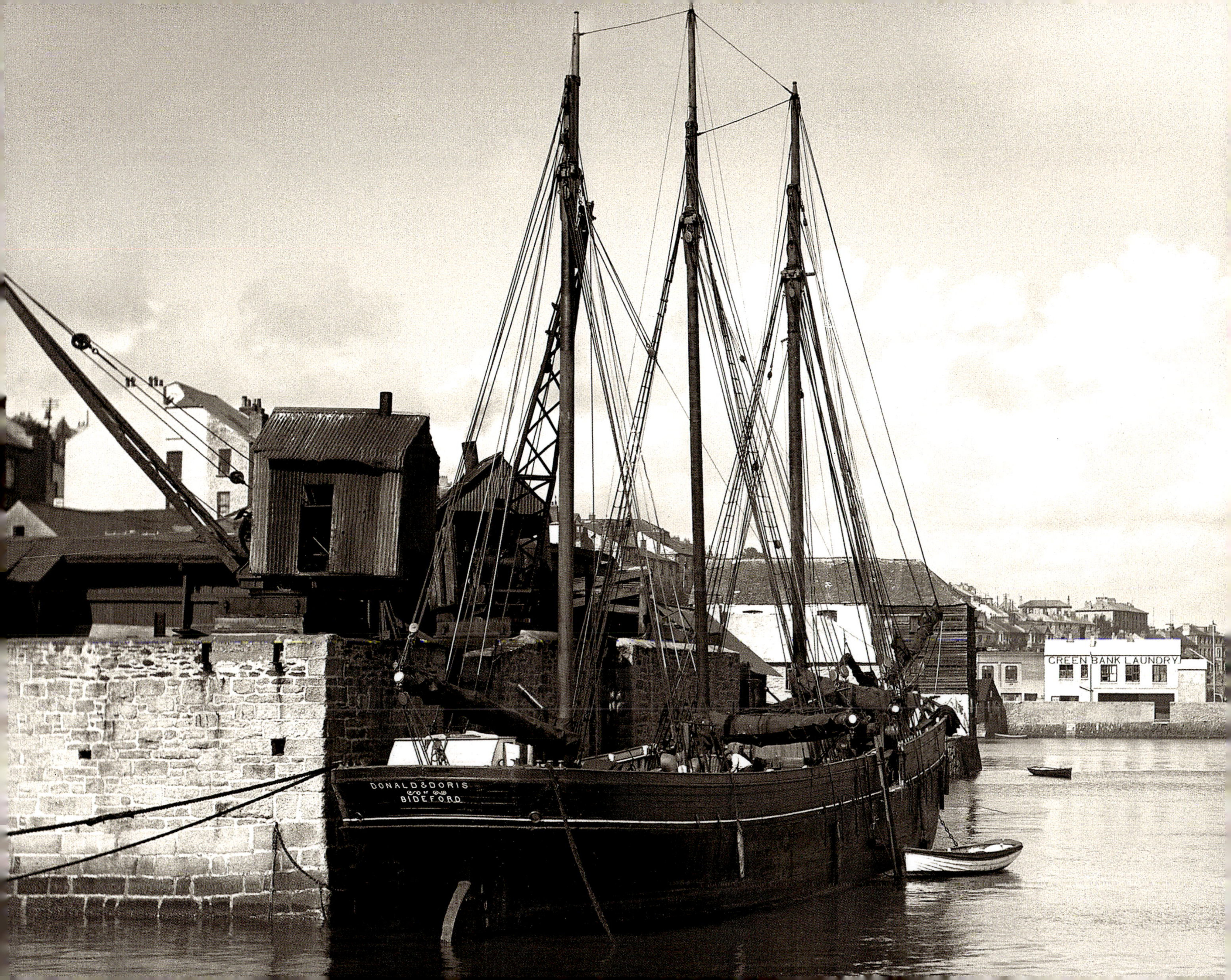
DONALD & DORIS
BIDEFORD
GREEN BANK LAUNDRY

Pilot Cutters & Gigs

Throughout the 1700s, up until the 1880s, steadily increasing numbers of vessels calling at Falmouth for orders, created a demand for local pilots – experience seamen who could guide these deep-water ships safely into the anchorage in Carrick Roads. Prior to the early 1800s these pilots were completely unregulated, and a cut-throat business developed in which the first pilot to board an inbound vessel got the job – which led to the development of fine lined, fast sailing cutters, to beat the competition. But, these craft had also to be weatherly enough to go seeking homeward-bounders in the Western Approaches, out as far as the Isles of Scilly.

Because of the potential risks of any seaman, or longshoreman, claiming to be a pilot, and an increasing number of vessels being lost in home waters, in the first decade of the nineteenth century the Corporation of Trinity House introduced Pilotage Districts around the coast of England and Wales. Coupled to the creation of these districts, was the introduction of a licensing scheme for pilots, who were examined by locally appointed commissioners to ascertain their capabilities. Even so the service remained unregulated in how the pilots behaved and sought new business.

We have little information about the Fal pilots prior to the introduction of the Trinity House pilotage districts. Since then, however, there have been frequent reports to Parliament, touching on the service. From these we know there have been over 40 sailing pilot boats employed over the years, with a maximum of thirteen and any at any one period being 13 between the 1860s, & 80s. Prior to the 1850s the pilot sloops and cutters were about 40 feet in length, measuring about 20 tons, their size increasing to just under 70 feet in the 1870s and 80s.

Pellew, lute stern
(Oil on linen. 2018. 150 x 120cm)

The stern of the *Pellew* in frame. This was the stage of construction she was at when I first visited Luke and his team of shipwrights in their new Rhoda Mary shipyard at Truro in 2017. The *Pellew* is due to be launched in February 2020.

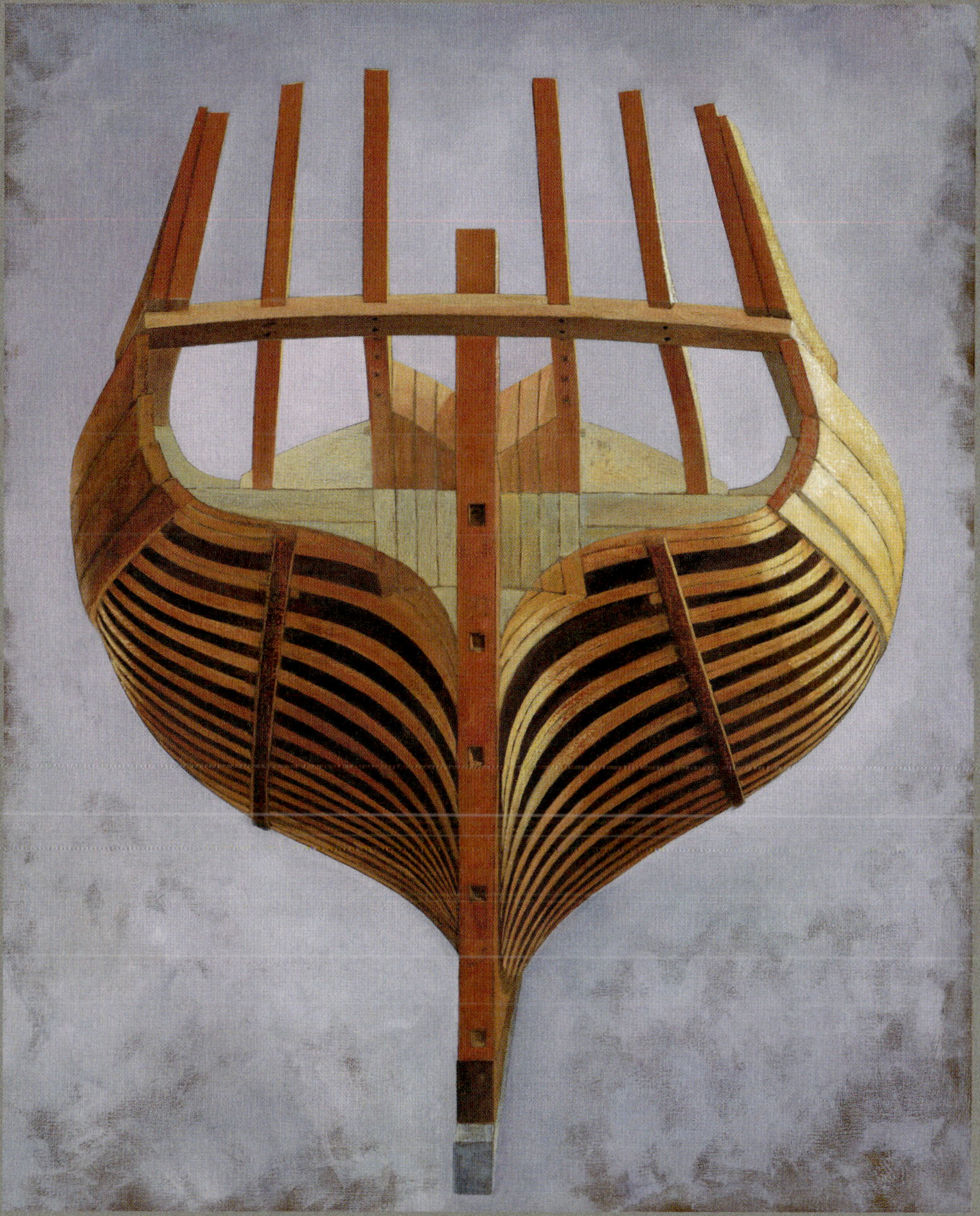

The St. Mawes and Falmouth communities each had distinct groups of pilots, working in competition with each other, and racing for employment in Falmouth Bay and off the Lizard. This state continued until 1887, when a reducing number of ships calling at Falmouth, led to the creation of the Falmouth and District Pilot Boat Association managed by a self-governing committee of management elected by the members. After the creation of the association in 1887, the number of active pilot cutters was quickly reduced to seven, and slowly decreased thereafter.

The ships they brought into port invariably lay at anchor in Carrick Roads throughout their stay, and rarely came alongside the quays. Even most of those discharging cargo in the port, did so at moorings, into a host of river barges.

Foreward Bulkhead, Pellew
(Oil on linen. 2018. 95 x 130cm)

This is before the decks were laid so the light was streaming in. It shows the crew's quarters in the foc'sle through what will become a water-tight door. I like to see the structure, which will soon disppear behind the saloon fittings.

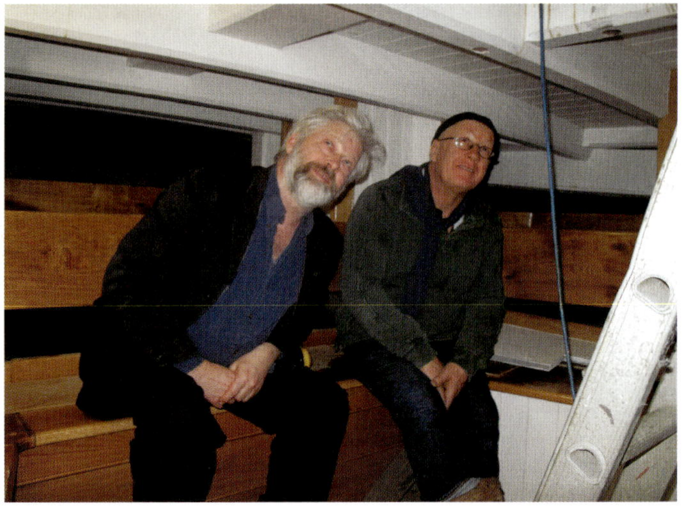

Luke and me in *Pellew's* captain's cabin.

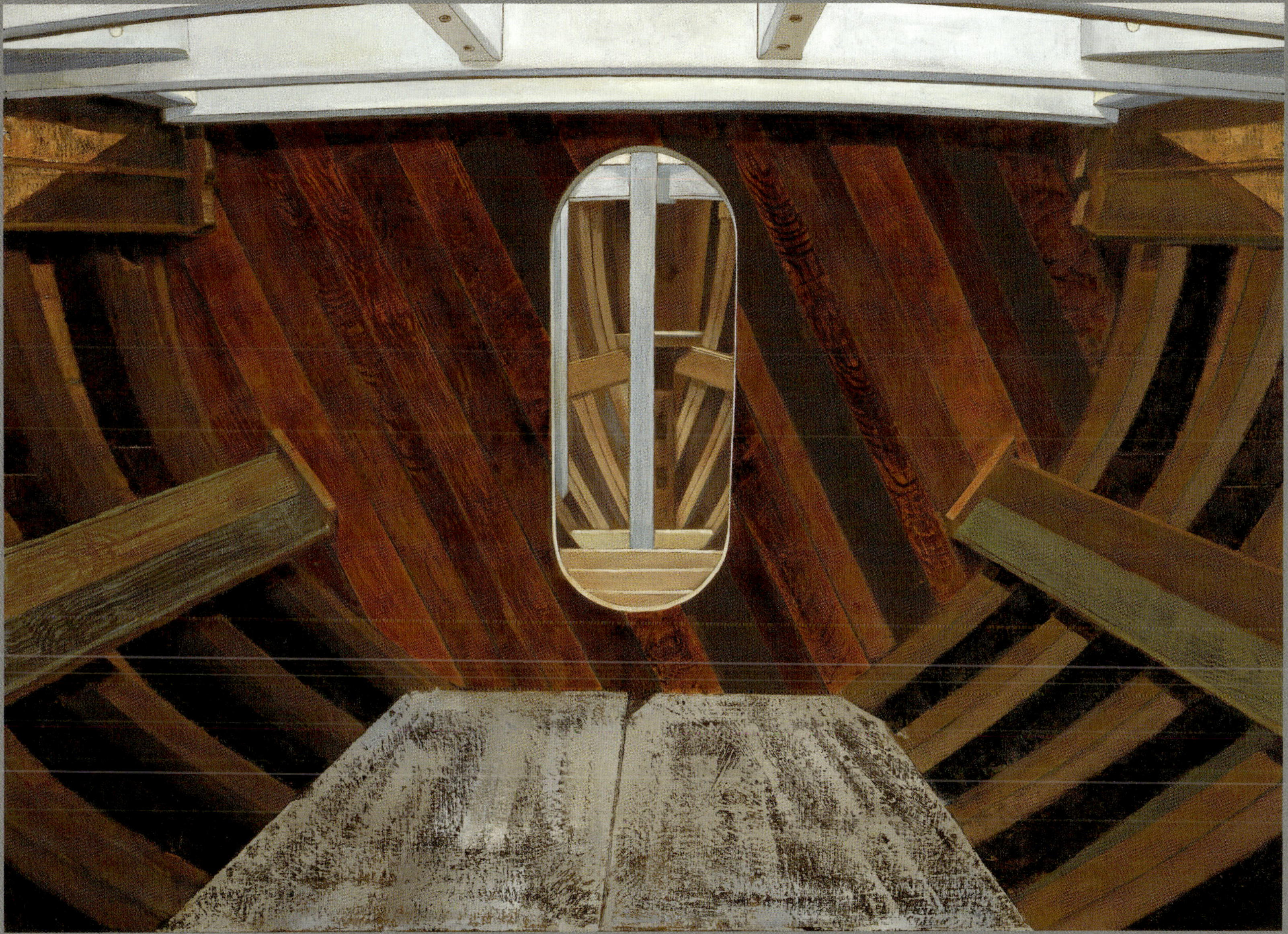

Nearer the shore, the same cut-throat pressures in the pilotage service led to the building of fine lined rowing gigs about 10 meters long, pulled by six oarsmen. In the late eighteenth century, anti-smuggling laws limited the number rowers permitted in these sleek craft five or less. But as the nineteenth century grew older, and organised smuggling became less of a problem for the authorities, these laws were repealed and six-oared Cornish pilot gig were common throughout the ports and harbour of the county. A few of the older gigs survived into the mid-1950s, when the competitive sport of gig racing came into vogue. Since the 1980s this sport has grown and grown with a great number of clubs and new gigs built to strictly controlled dimensions and specifications, to ensure as near as possible an equality in the boats, leaving the competitive element to the skill and power of the rowers. Gig races are now a very popular feature of local regattas.

Outfitters' Cutters

In parallel with the pilot cutters, a similar style of smaller cutters were adopted by the 'outfitters,' the tailors and haberdashers of the town. They plied for trade amongst the homeward bound ships off the port. Invariably young men, who went to sea as callow youths, came home from long voyages of a year as strapping seamen, unable to fit into their original shore-going clothes. The outfitters would board in-bound ships on the way into Carrick Roads, measure as many of the crew as would engage with them, and have a new made suit of clothes ready for them before their ships sailed for their final port of discharge.

Pilot Gig
(Oil on linen. 2018. 90 x 150cm)

Faith, from the Devoran Pilot Gig Club based at Restronguet Creek, near Falmouth. The rebirth of the pilot gig is due in great extent to Ralph Bird the boatbuilder. In 1991 Mr. Bird built a gig for his own village of Devoran. It was called the *Fear Not* named after an earlier historic Devoran gig. 28 more gigs for other clubs followed. All modern racing gigs are based on the *Treffry*, built in 1838 by Williams Peters in St. Mawes and survives to this day.

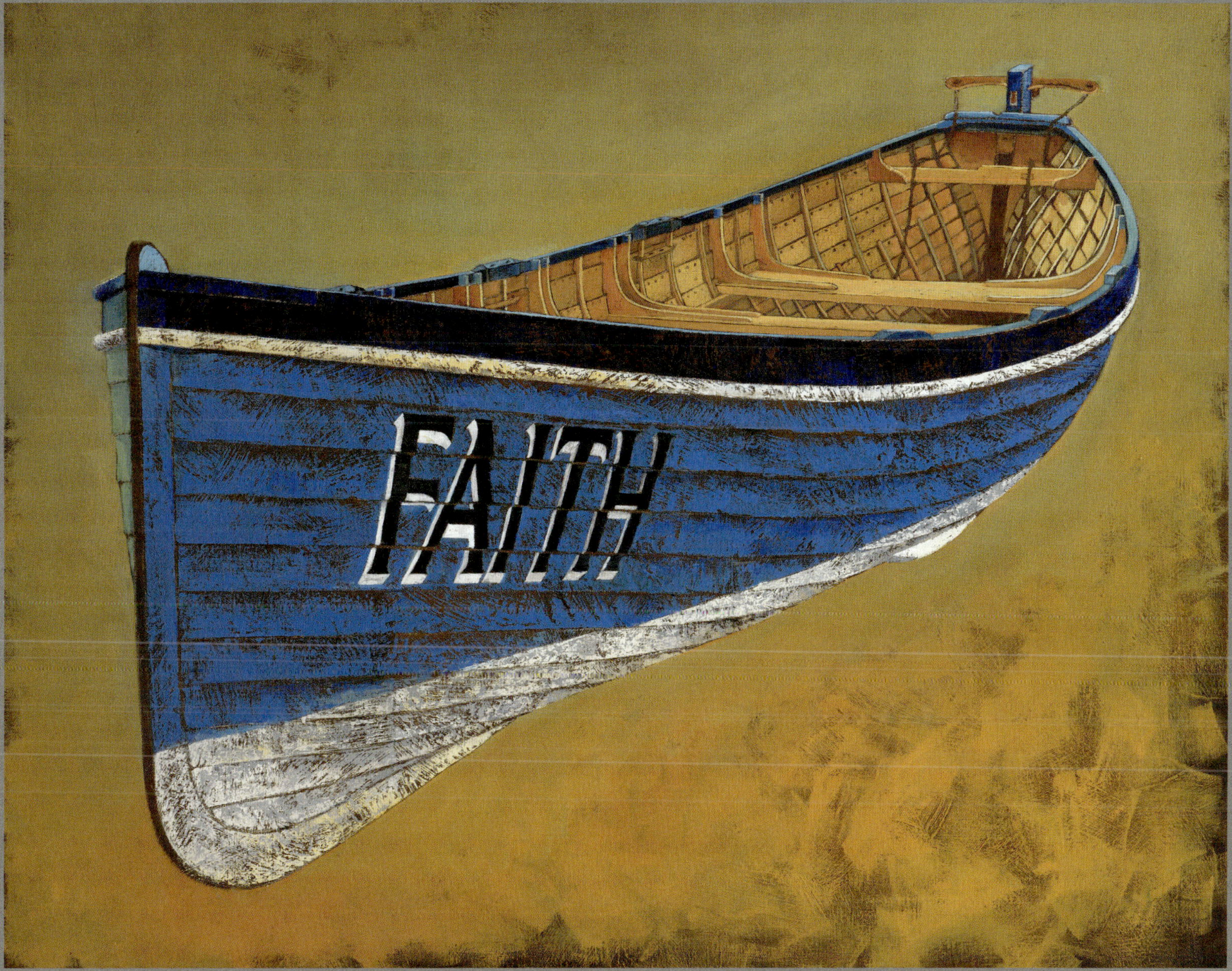
FAITH

Quay Punts

A third level of service under sail was offered by the smaller Quay Punts, thought even these would go seeking for business well down the bay off the Lizard. Manned by one or two men, these boats were effectively the water taxis; the grocery vans; and the liberty bots. Once engaged by a captain, they would attend his ship throughout her stay in Falmouth, carrying the master to and from shore on ship's business with the agents, bringing out fresh provisions, and carrying crew members to and from the shore if leave was permitted.

After the First World War the commercial employment opportunities for quay punts fell dramatically, but the design if these craft, with their long keels, easy sail-plan, and sea-keeping abilities, proved very popular with yachtsmen operating on modest budgets. Through the 1920s and 30s, old Falmouth Quay Punts were converted into yachts, and new craft along the same lines were designed and built in good numbers in the local yards.

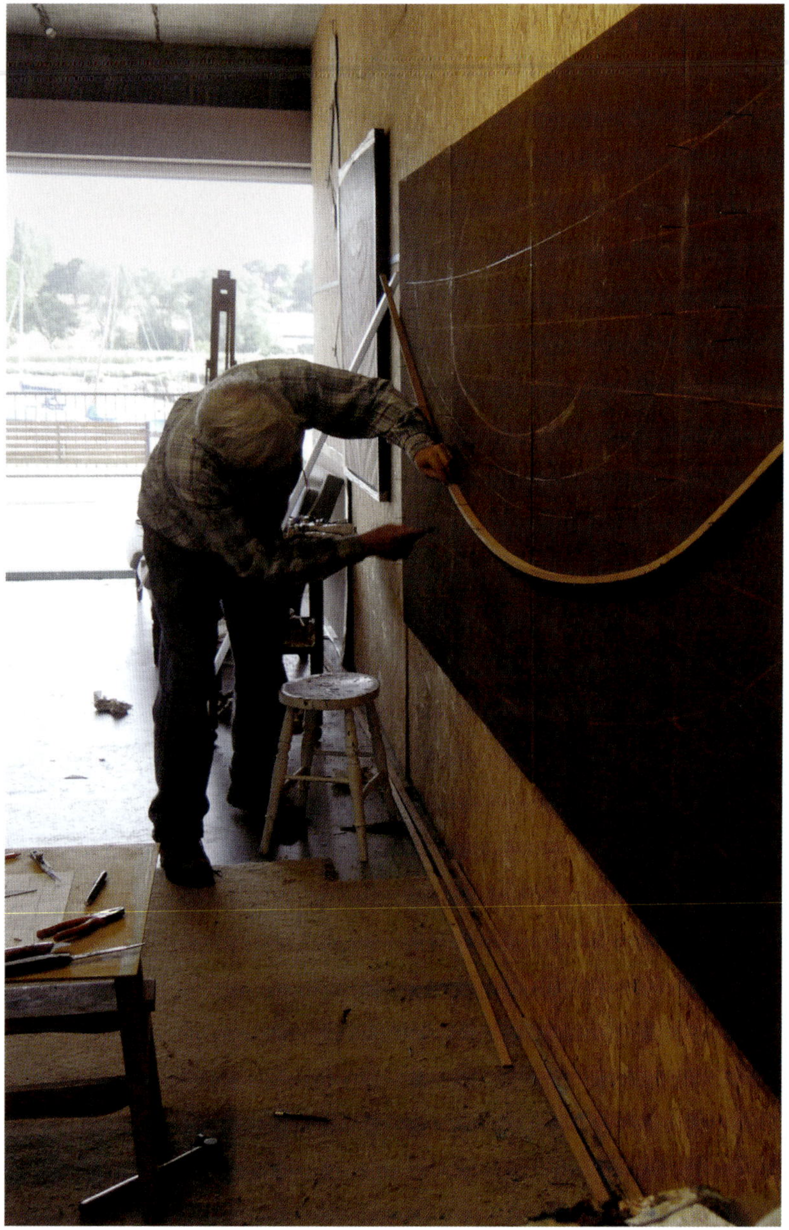

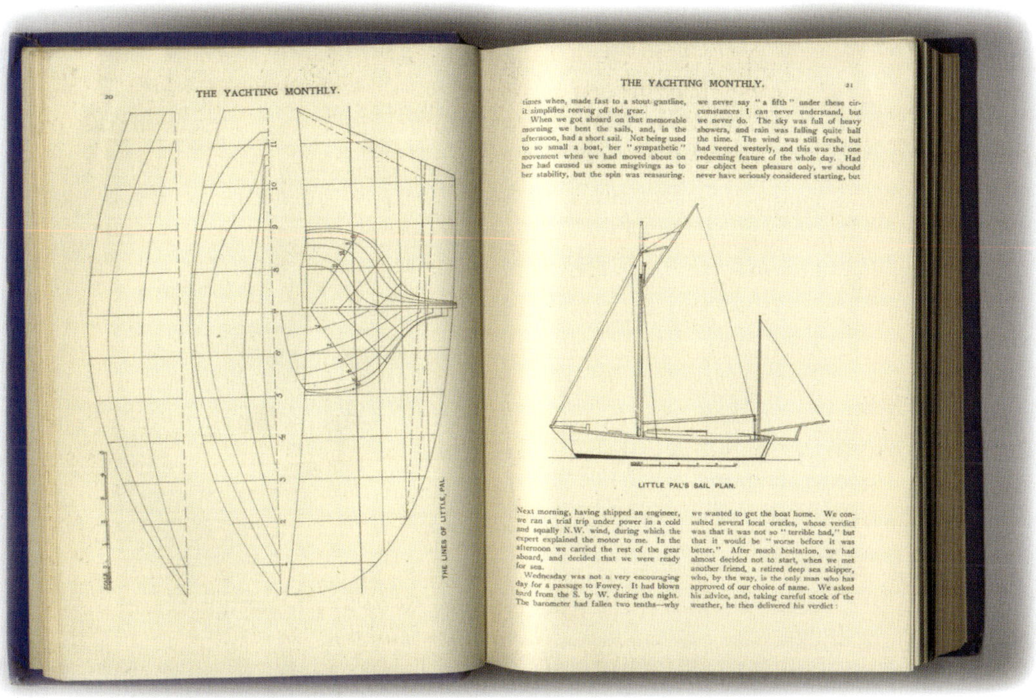
20 THE YACHTING MONTHLY.

THE LINES OF LITTLE PAL.

THE YACHTING MONTHLY. 21

times when, made fast to a stout gantline, it simplifies reeving off the gear.

When we got aboard on that memorable morning we bent the sails, and, in the afternoon, had a short sail. Not being used to so small a boat, her "sympathetic" movement when we had moved about on her had caused us some misgivings as to her stability, but the spin was reassuring.

LITTLE PAL'S SAIL PLAN.

Next morning, having shipped an engineer, we ran a trial trip under power in a cold and squally N.W. wind, during which the expert explained the motor to me. In the afternoon we carried the rest of the gear aboard, and decided that we were ready for sea.

Wednesday was not a very encouraging day for a passage to Fowey. It had blown hard from the S. by W. during the night. The barometer had fallen two tenths—why we never say "a fifth" under these circumstances I can never understand, but we never do. The sky was full of heavy showers, and rain was falling quite half the time. The wind was still fresh, but had veered westerly, and this was the one redeeming feature of the whole day. Had our object been pleasure only, we should never have seriously considered starting, but we wanted to get the boat home. We consulted several local oracles, whose verdict was that it was not so "terrible bad," but that it would be "worse before it was better." After much hesitation, we had almost decided not to start, when we met another friend, a retired deep sea skipper, who, by the way, is the only man who has approved of our choice of name. We asked his advice, and, taking careful stock of the weather, he then delivered his verdict:

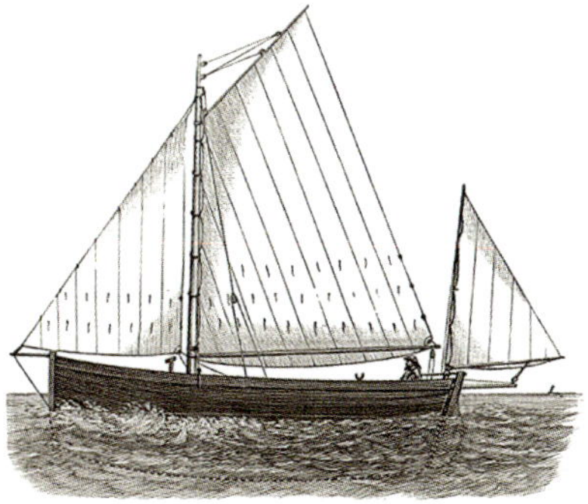

Yachting Monthly 1915
A Quay Punt built for yachting with a taller rig. The working rig of a punt was shorter (see above), it is said, to be able to fit under the yardarm of a ship when going alongside. And also better in bad weather conditions.

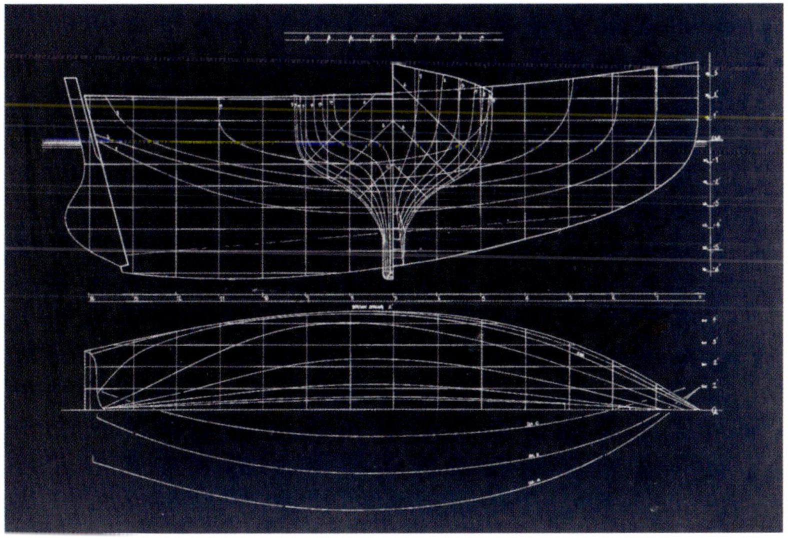

The *Curlew,* now part of the museum's collection. The Quay Punt has proved to a very sea-worthy little vessel. After being rebuilt with a double skin of planking the *Curlew* made the historic voyage with Tim & Pauline Carr to South Georgia and even over-wintered there. The celebrated yacht designer Uffa Fox in 1926 sang the praises of the Falmouth quay punt *Twilight,* sailing her from Norway to Cowes, a 'stormy passage'. 'I had no fears as to her seaworthiness and ability to take what came in the way of weather.'

(next page)

Falmouth Quay Punt, Curlew
(Oil on 4 gesso boards. 2018. 137 x 366cm)

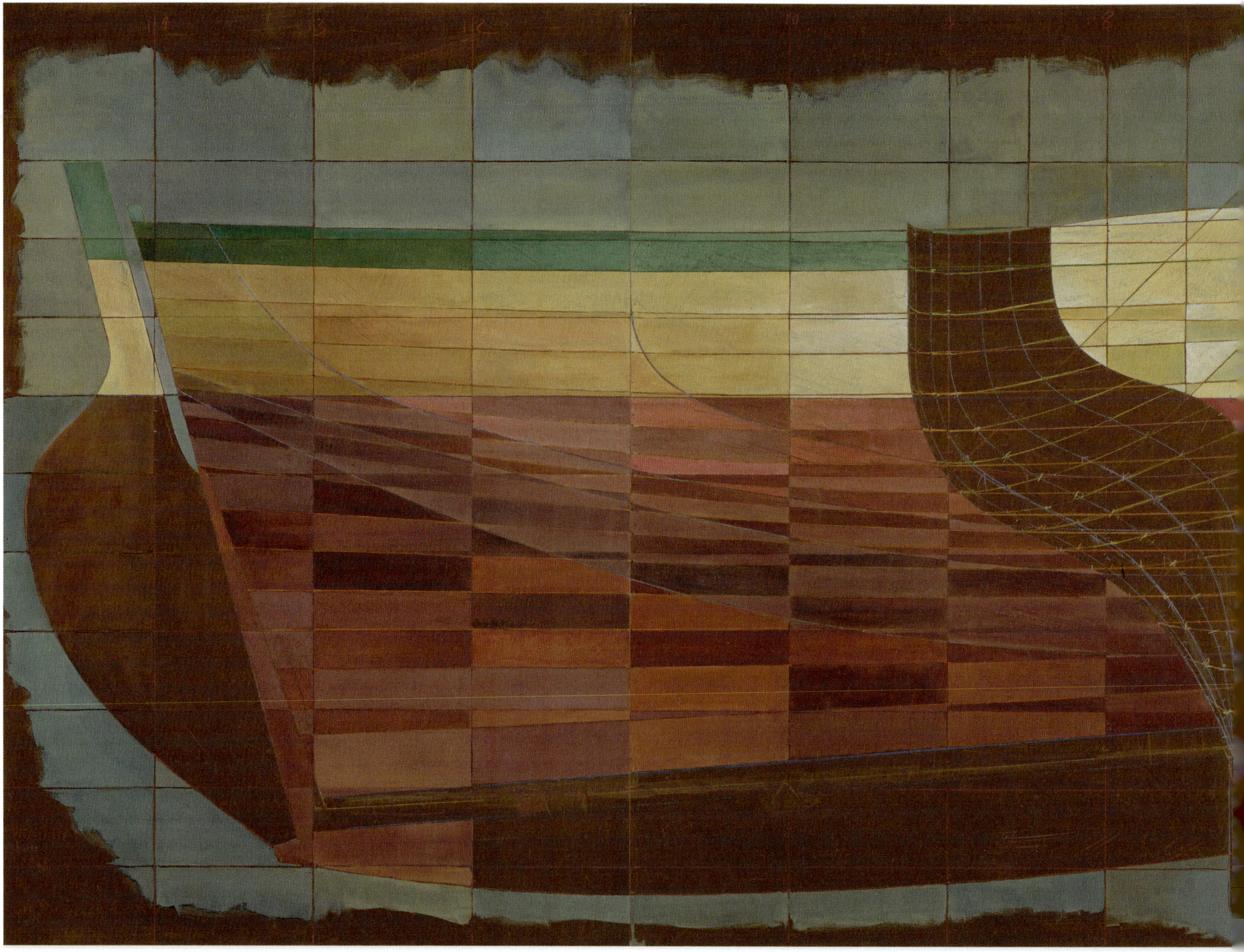

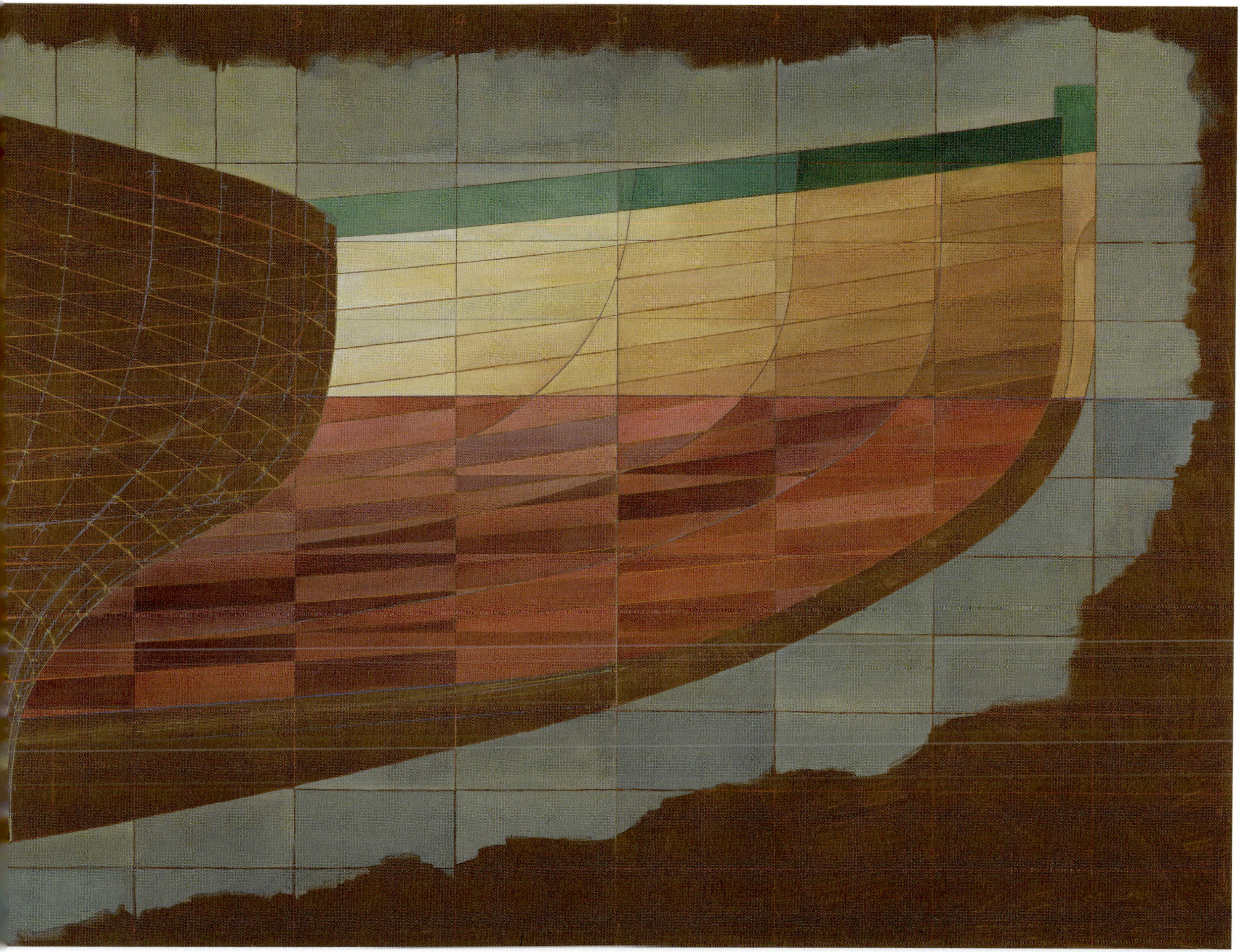

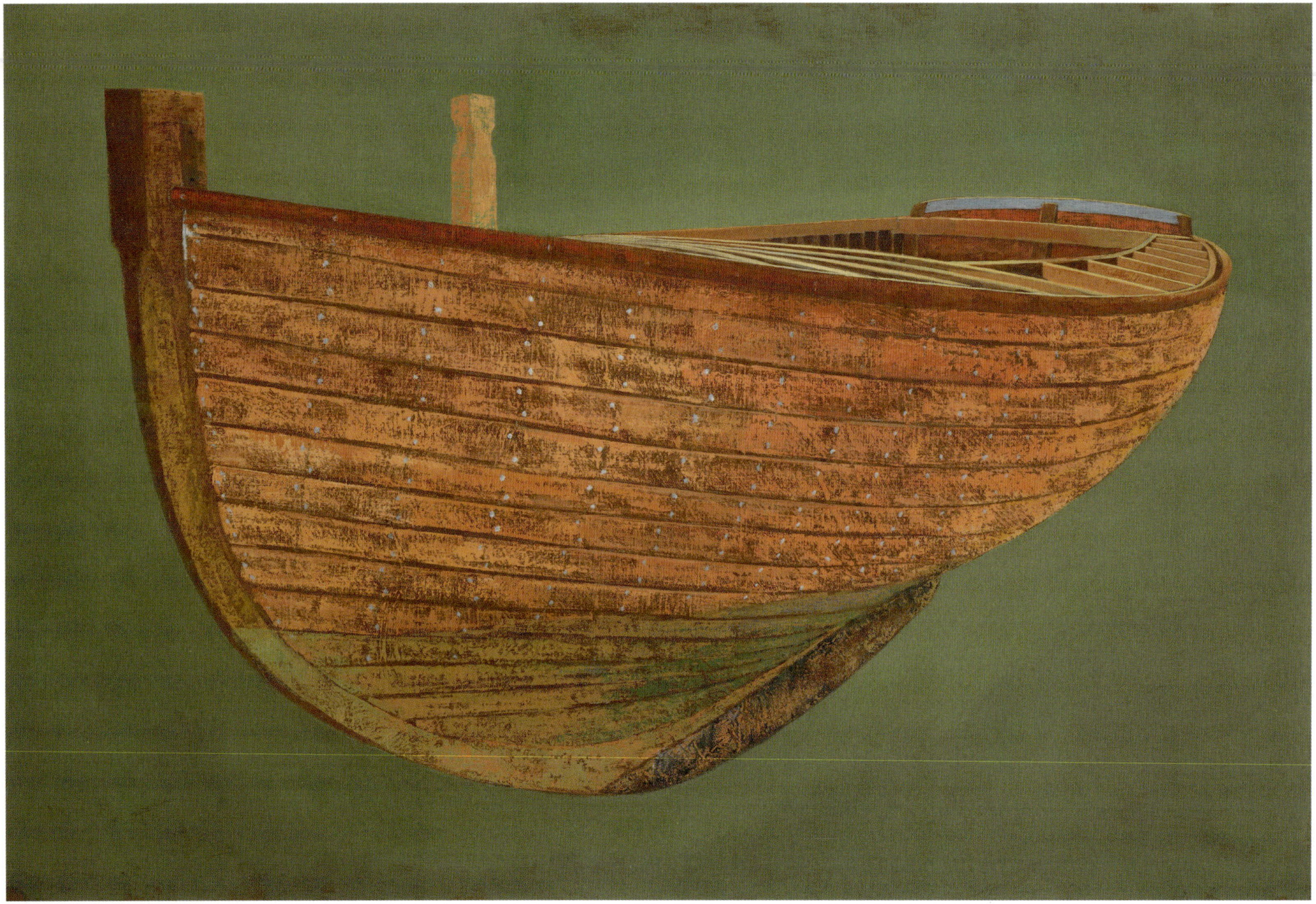

Falmouth Quay Punt
(Oil on linen. 2018. 90 x 130cm)

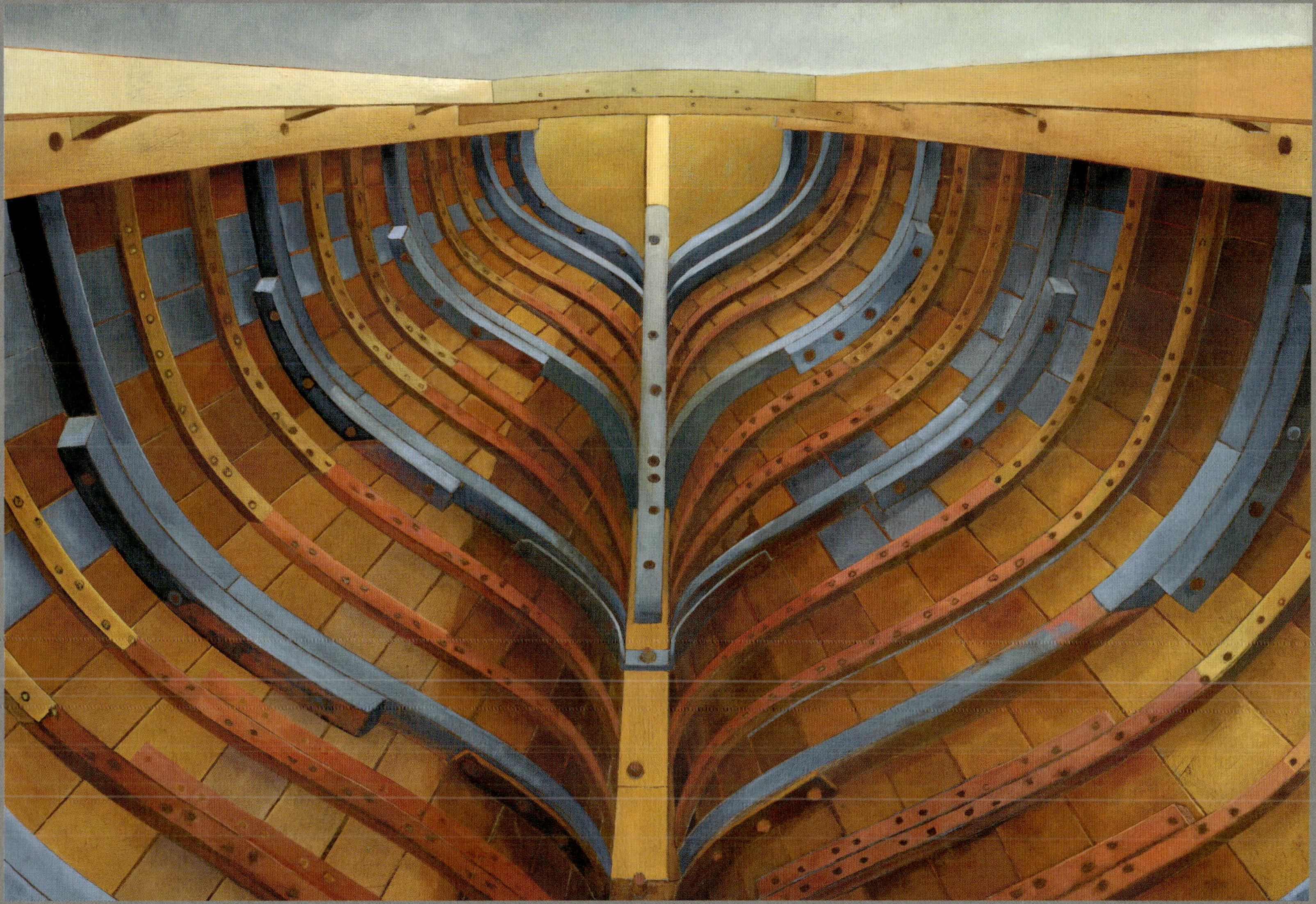

Falmouth Quay Punt looking aft
(Oil on linen. 2018. 90 x 130cm)

Watermen's boats

Small rowing boats, usually manned by one man, they would scurry round picking up casual business moving small numbers of people and/or commodities around the harbour and the adjoining creeks. Prior to the creation of the Falmouth harbour authority in 1870 these craft were unregulated, and many operated on the fringes of legal trade. After 1870 they became licensed, and their behaviour was regulated by bye-laws. Their number peaked around the turn of the century with over a hundred men and boats so employed.

Fishing and Fishing Boats

Loosely the different kinds of fishing boats working from the Fal, fell into two sorts – inshore and offshore fishing boats. The inshore boats mainly comprised those employed in the oyster fishery – 'Working Boats,' and rowing boats variously referred to as 'Haul-tow Punts,' 'Wink Boats,' 'River Boats,' or 'Oyster Boats,' depending on which part of the river you worked; 'Seine-boats,' employed in the traditional Cornish pilchard fishery; and small hand-line fishing boats.

[*Irene*, a Haul-tow Punt hangs in the main gallery]

The offshore boats engaged in the pilchard, herring and mackerel drift fisheries, long-lining, and trawl fisheries for 'white fish.'

A view of the Town Quay at Falmouth showing a three-masted schooner, a cutter rigged smack and three Penzance motorised luggers:
PZ.131 *Ivy;*
PZ.119 *Hopeful;*
PZ.144 *Snowflake.*
Schooner *Mary Miller*
Kingsbridge smack *JNR*

Taken circa 1920s. *Cutty Sark* visible in the background, apparently restored as a full rigged ship. Horse and cart visible on quay, to take away cargo. (Bateman reference 230)

This photograph inspired my linocut of the quay.

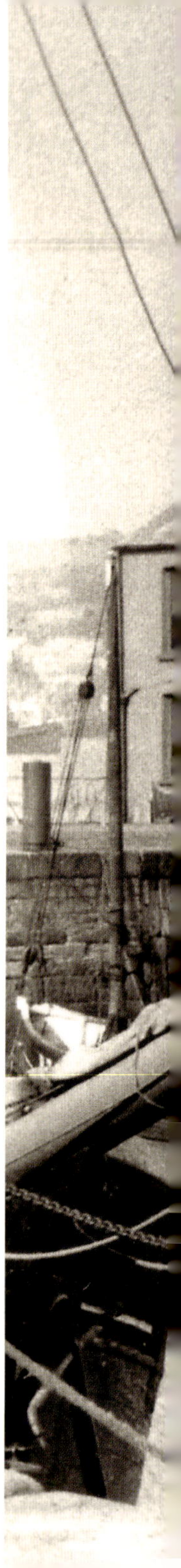

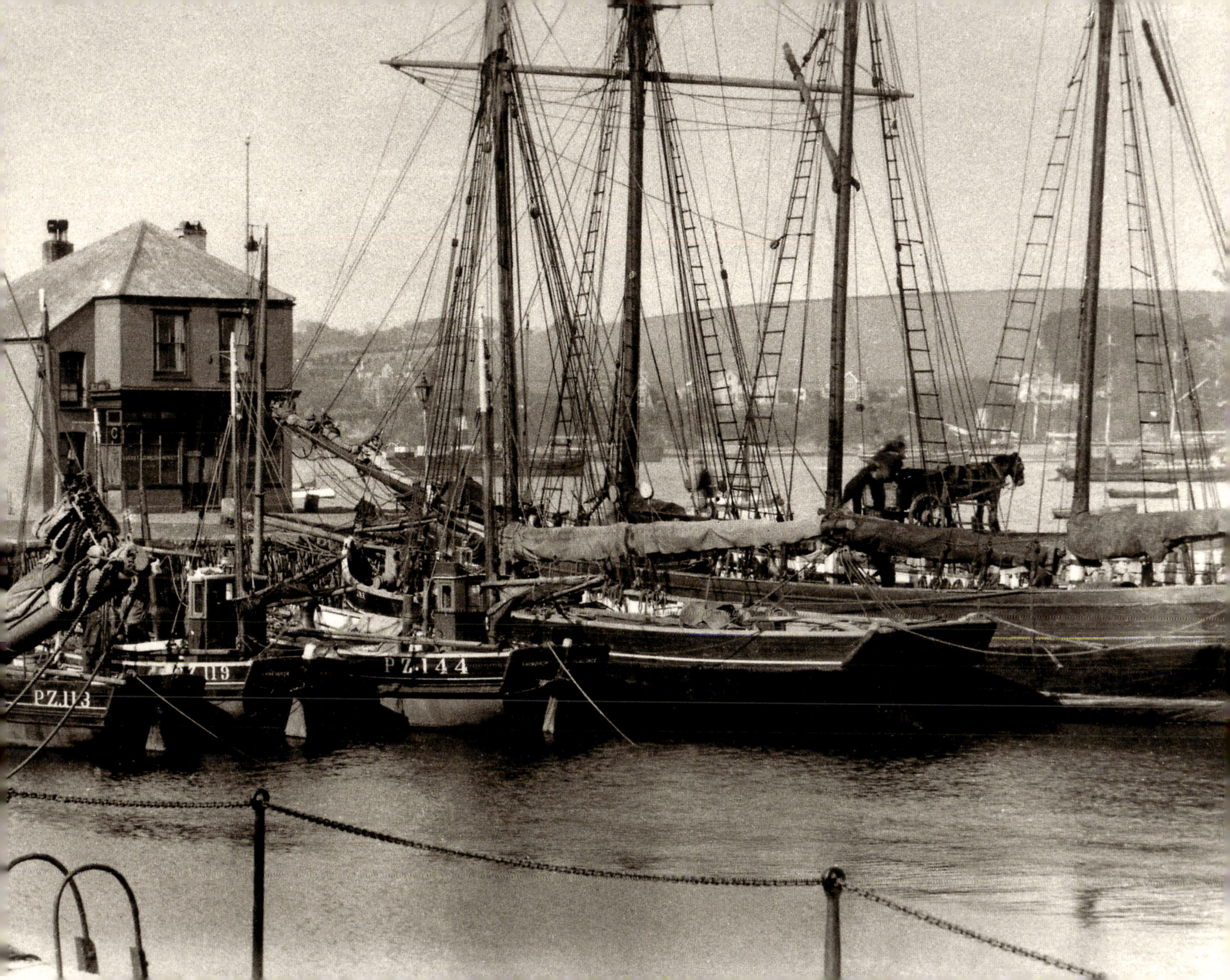
PZ.113
PZ.144

Working Boats

Within the 'port' of Falmouth and the confines of the River Fal, a class of sailing boats known ubiquitously as 'working boats,' were, and are, employed in the Fal Native Oyster fishery. For a variety of reasons, many related to the limited finances of the fishermen, these boats had no common design. Nor were many of them specifically built for the work. Many were adapted from second hand craft. Working over the mud, sand and shingle banks within the estuary, a relatively shallow draft was essential, as was the ability to hold a true course, under a balanced sail plan, needing a minimum of rudder work. These boats were crewed by up to three men working one, two or three oyster-dredges. Of ancient origins, boats, dredges and fishermen are now licensed, but in the early years the fishery was unregulated and the men fished in any month with an 'r' in it. In later years, after over-fishing had seriously depleted the stocks, the fishing season was shortened lopping off the months of September and April. Today the Fal Oyster fishing season runs from October to March, and fishing is permitted Mondays to Fridays, between 9 a.m., and 3 p.m., and on Saturdays between 9 a.m., and 1 p.m. The engagement in this fishery is strictly restricted to licensed sailing craft alone – though motors are now permitted for the passage to and from the oyster banks – and it is regulated by local authority bye-laws, the compliance with which is overseen by a water bailiff. A minimum size of oysters permitted to be landed is determined by their not being able to pass through an Oyster ring, or Oyster Gauge – a local authority stamped metal ring 67 mm. in diameter.

Originally timber built, today many are GRP craft. While the numbers actually engaged in fishing today are relatively small, many others based on similar designs, with their snazzy gaff-topsails, are recreational boats which race evenings and weekends throughout the summer.

Working Boat Endeavour looking aft
(Oil on linen. 2018. 90 x 110cm)

Thanks to Ollie Graffy, naval architect and the owner of *Endeavour*.

The boats that are still dredging oysters have a working rig which is replaced with larger spars and sails for racing in the summer, but a large number of these boats are now sailed purely for pleasure and very competitively raced.

(Falmouth Working Boats Association: fwba.co.uk)

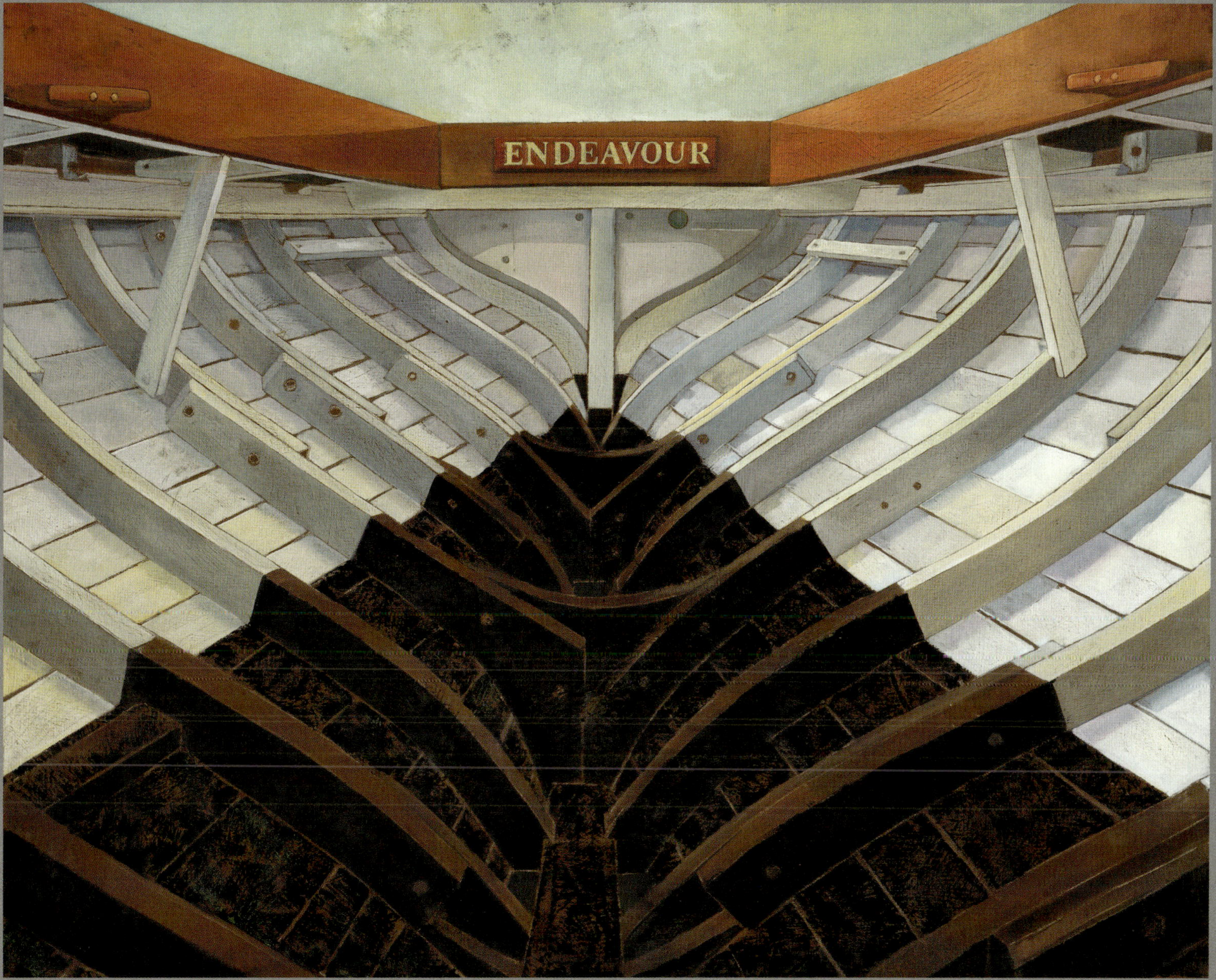
ENDEAVOUR

‘Haul-tow Punts,’ ‘Wink Boats,’ ‘River Boats,’ or ‘Oyster Boats’

Secondary to the working boats engaged in the oyster fishery were and are river skiffs or punts, rowing boats usually worked by one man. Men and boats are licensed, and were loosely known as ‘Haul-tow Punts,’ ‘Wink Boats,’ ‘River Boats,’ or ‘Oyster Boats’ on different parts of the river. The term Haul-tow punts, often pronounced ‘aulto punts, is a derivative term culled from their mode of working – by hauling on the anchor line while towing the dredge astern across the oyster beds. The traditional punts were usually carvel built, sturdy but lightweight craft of from 13 to 16 ft in length, with a broad transom stern, and were notionally rated at one ton. A two drum winch/ windlass system, or ‘wink,’ is mounted as close to the bows as the beam of the boat will allow. Simple locking pins enable either drum to be worked independently, or to free-wheel. A table or ‘cultch board’ fitted across the stern serves for landing the dredge and sorting the catch.

Usually worked in calm conditions, or in the upper reaches of the Fal, most Haul-tow punts only worked one dredge over the stern. Very occasionally two dredges were worked, one over each quarter, but of 148 boats licensed in 1924, only 3 worked two dredges.

To maximise their fishing ability, the dredges used were of the largest practical size. One of eighteen rings across the knife being about the largest employed.

Out of season these boats used to serve as market boats carrying fresh fruit and vegetable produce from riverside orchards and small-holdings, to markets in Falmouth, Truro and Penryn, but today the orchards and small-holdings have largely been abandoned.

In the twenty first century only a handful of hardy fishermen seasonally engage in this work.

New floors and frames in a Falmouth Working Boat
(Oil on linen. 2018. 90 x 120cm)

This was the Falmouth Working Boat *Bluebell* who I painted several times in 2013 while she was being rebuilt on the East Coast. The large floor timbers are probably larger than she was built with. I like to do paintings that show the boat’s structure before it is fitted out.

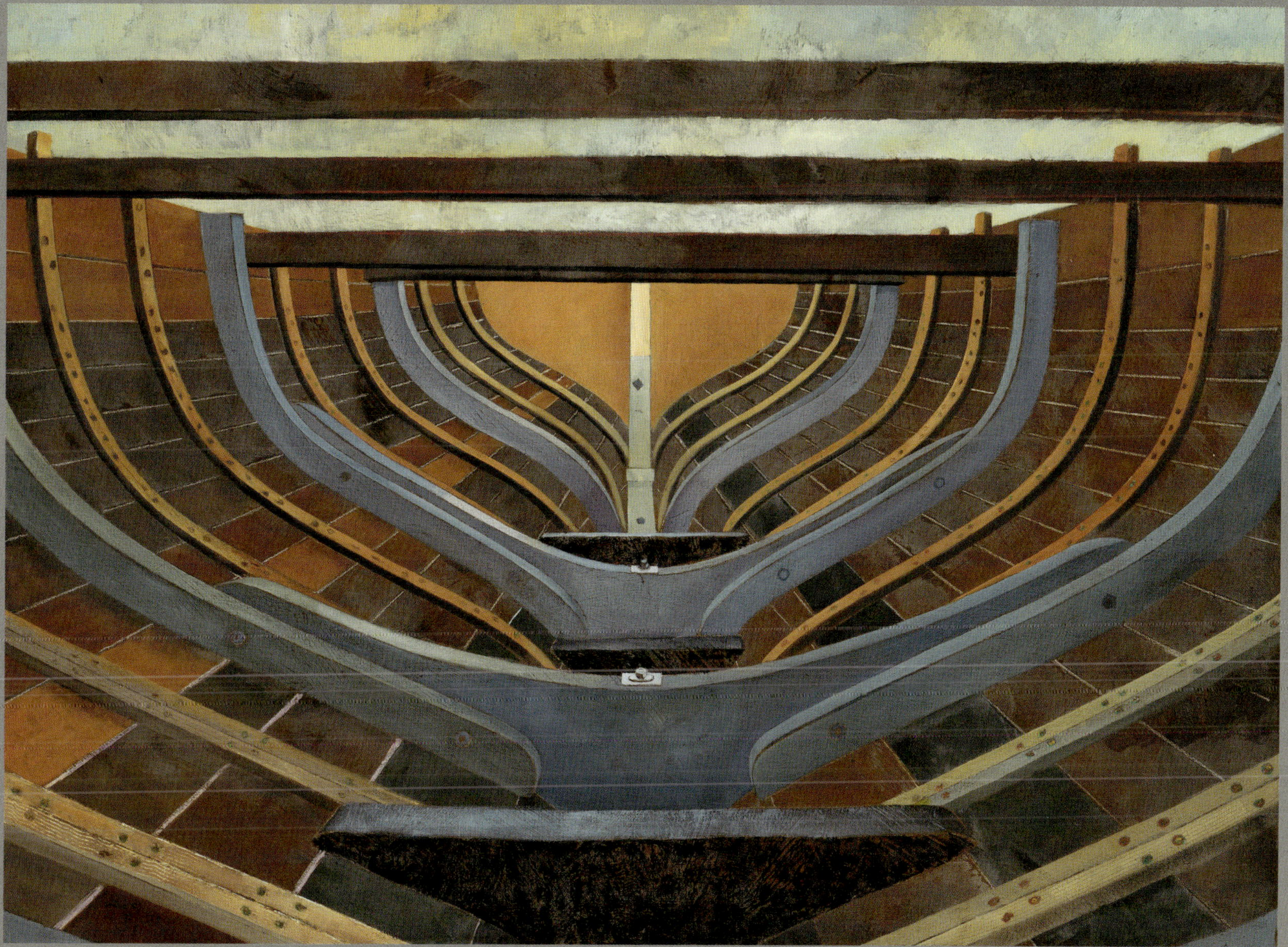

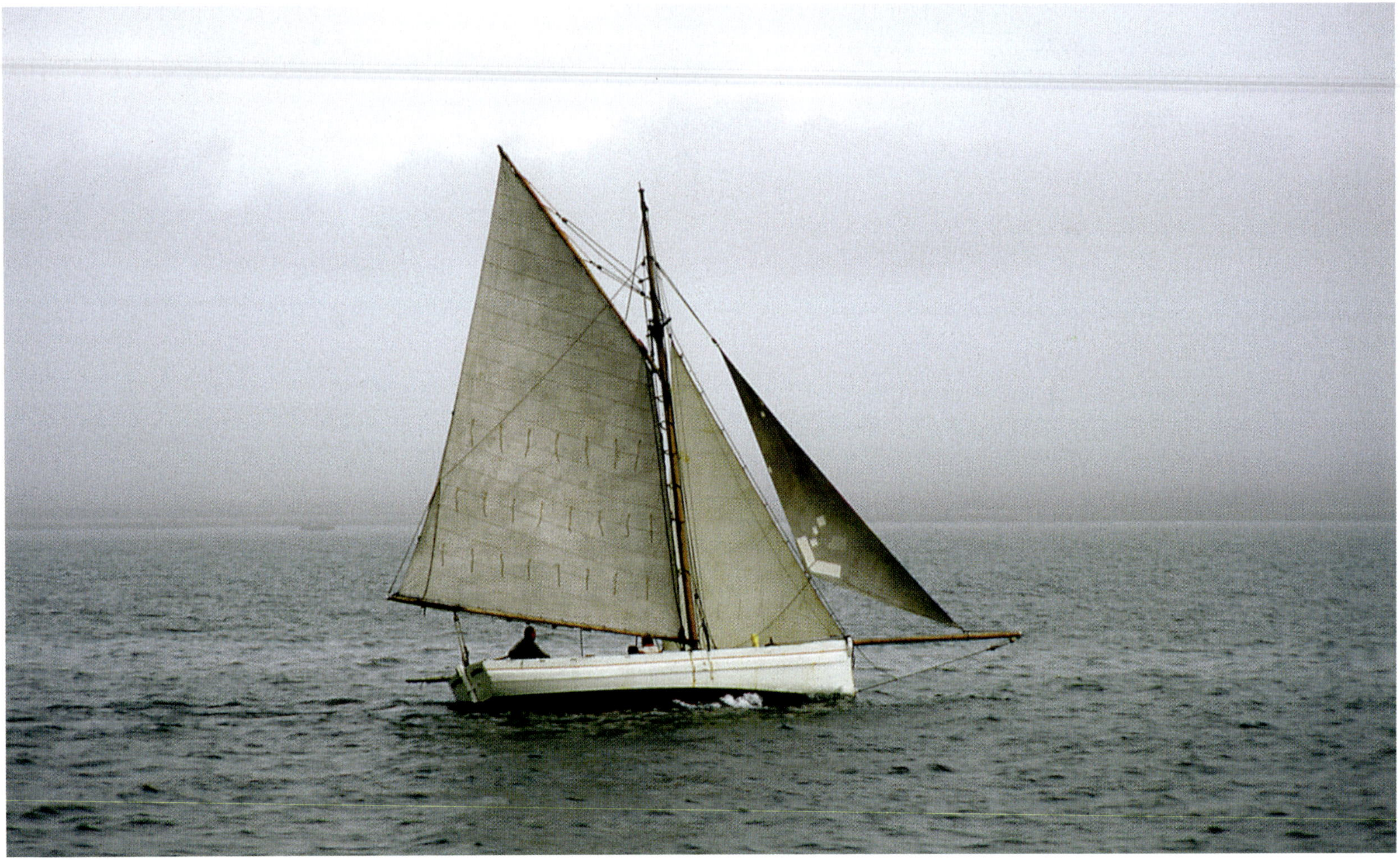

View of an unknown cutter in Falmouth Harbour, possibly an Oyster Dredger. Taken from the St. Mawes ferry during September 1964.

Falmouth Working Boat
(Oil on linen. 2018. 90 x 130cm)

I fell in love with the shape of this beautiful little working boat, high and dry on Mylor beach. She was in a sorry state, a few planks missing with seaweed hanging from her rails. I hope someone with deep pockets will rebuild her one day. I later found out that this boat is the *Shadow* built in 1884 and fund raising to re-build her is indeed underway. She was dredging oysters up to 2013 and is thought to be the oldest surviving working boat.

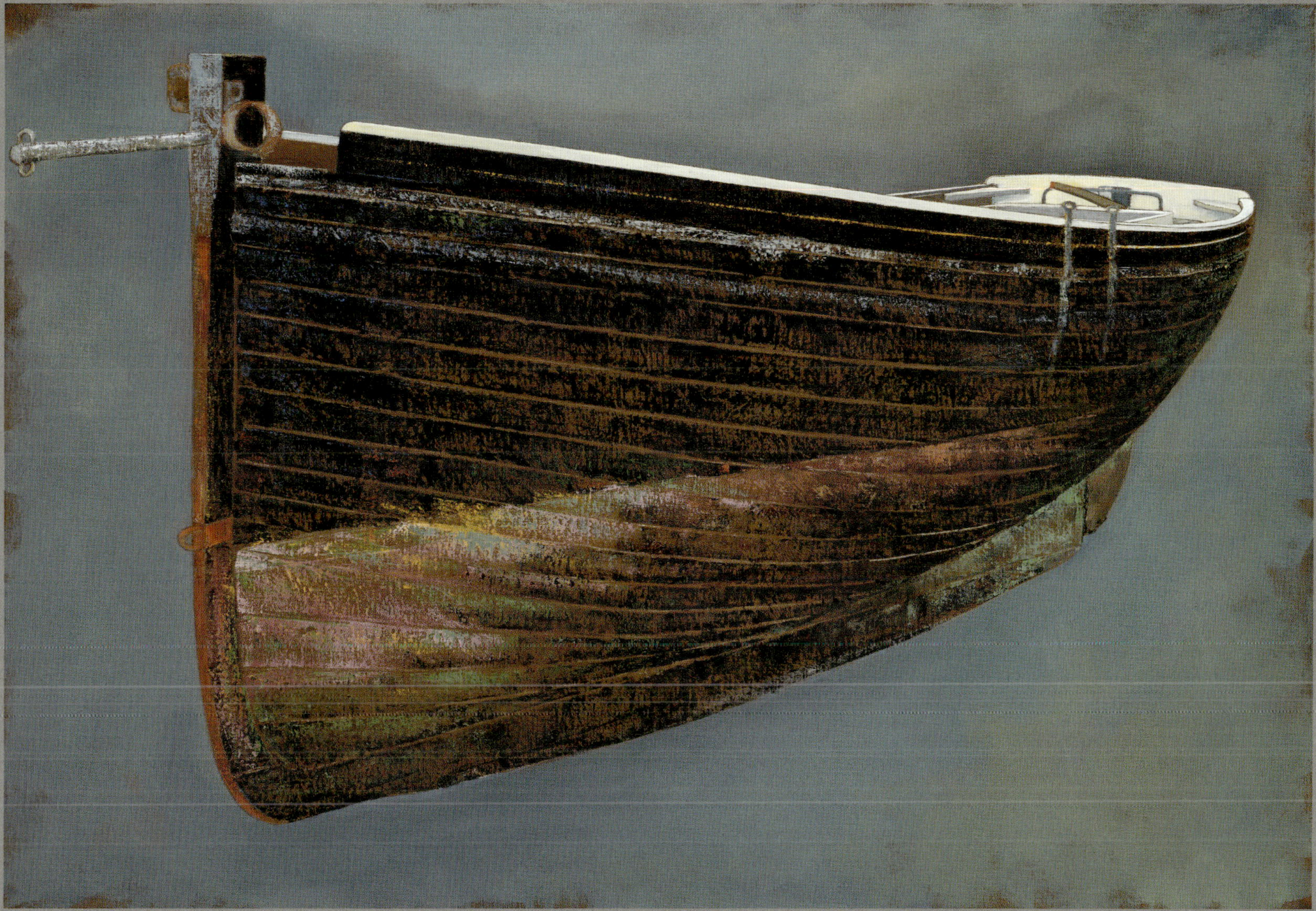

Seine boats

For many centuries seine fishing was the principal means of catching Cornish pilchards for commercial markets. Now long discontinued, in the seine-net fishery a lengthy curtain of net was used to encircle shoals of pilchards as they came close to the shore. Relatively expensive to fit out and maintain, the seine fishery was carried on by numerous companies of financial speculators, and each concern usually owned three boats of different sizes and purpose. The 'seine boats,' carried a great seine some hundreds of yards in length, which was shot around a shoal of pilchards. They were mostly carvel built, open boats, of about 30 feet in length, and carried a crew of five or six men. The 'volyers,' or 'followers,' tended to be clinker built, open-boats, carrying a 'stop seine,' which could be shot across the mouth of the great seine top ensure the catch was securely enclosed. These were attended by a 'lurcher,' or 'lurker,' which carried the seine master who directed operations afloat. Once a shoal was securely enclosed, and moored, the pilchards could be kept alive within the confines of the seine net for several days, during which manageable quantities were drawn out of the shoal each day for curing in the pilchard cellars, on shore.

Mackerel drivers

Decked, lug sailed fishing boats of the largest Cornish class, engaged in the drift fisheries. Of 40 to 50 feet in length, they were based mainly in Newlyn, Mousehole & Porthleven [Penzance], St. Ives, and Fowey, working under the respective port registration letters of PZ, SS, & FY. Only a few boats of this class worked out of Falmouth, under the FH, registration. The mackerel drivers, which were notionally worked by crews of seven men, or six men and a boy, were mainly employed in the great Spring Mackerel Fishery, off the coast of Cornwall, which extended from February to June, each year. Working up to 80 miles off-shore, they supplied the daily fresh-fish markets catering for the metropolitan markets of London and midland cities.

Out of season many of these boats and crews also engaged in the Irish, and North Sea herring fisheries, their crew living on board for weeks at a time, while working out of distant harbours.

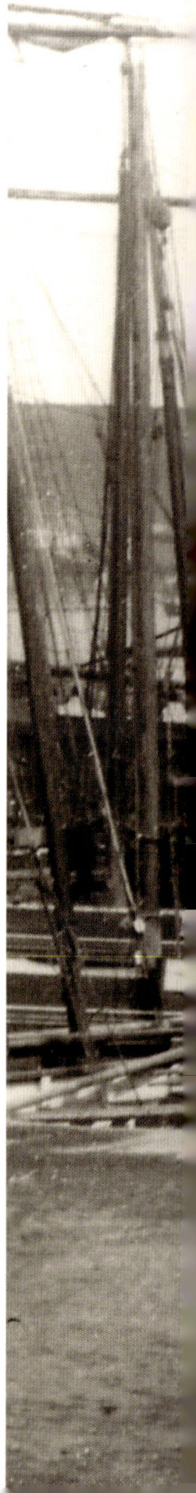

View of the inner basin at Custom House Quay, Falmouth, full of Penzance registered fishing boats – mostly Porthleven mackerel drivers, including:
PZ.424 *Beatie;*
PZ.271 *Industry;*
PZ.593 *Our Boys;*
and PZ.316 *Agnes Weston*
Taken circa 1920(?). Bateman reference 36.

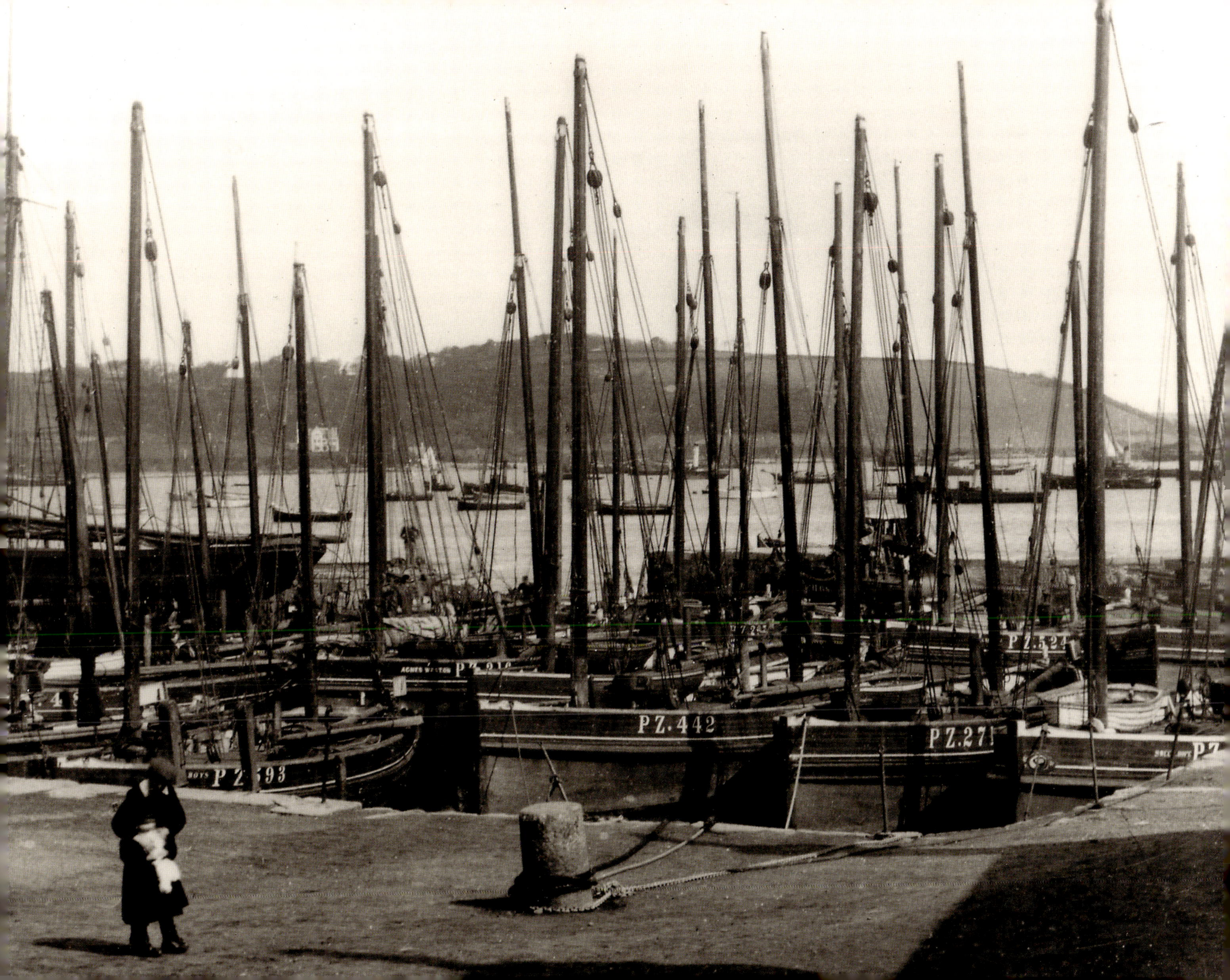
PZ.442
PZ.271

Pilchard drivers

Were smaller lug sailed drift fishing boats, of from 20 to 30 feet in length, and included open boats, and half-decked boats. Employed in the summer and autumn Cornish pilchard fisheries, they were crewed by two to five men, and/or boys, sailing out of port each evening, and returning during the early hours of the next morning – wind and weather permitting.

Most were laid-up out of season, though some engaged in thee crab and lobster fisheries, and hand-line fishing.

Long-liners

Long-lining was introduced as an alternative mode of fishing, for local mackerel drivers, driven out of that fishery by the mass arrival of East Coast steam drifters in the first decade of the nineteen hundreds. This mode of fishing was further developed with the introduction of marine internal combustion engines in the west, from about 1910. With these boats the hull form was gradually modified from pure sailing lines to a power driven shape.

Beach boats – Crabbers and Hand-liners

Mainly small open boats, worked by sail and oar, whose forms were adapted to suit specific local conditions. All quite similar in general, but with particular quirks of design arising in different coves.

For constructional information on most of the following craft generally see my contribution to The CHATHAM Directory of Inshore Craft, London, 1997 [ISBN 1 86176 029 9]; pages 145-177.

St Ives Lugger
(Oil on linen. 2018. 95 x 90cm)

One of two little St. Ives Luggers built by Jonny Nance for the St. Ives Jumbo Association (stivesjumbo.com).

'Jumbos were a class of fishing boat introduced uniquely to St. Ives during the mid 1880s by the renowned boatbuilder, William Paynter.' This boat has been named in honour of the orginal builder.

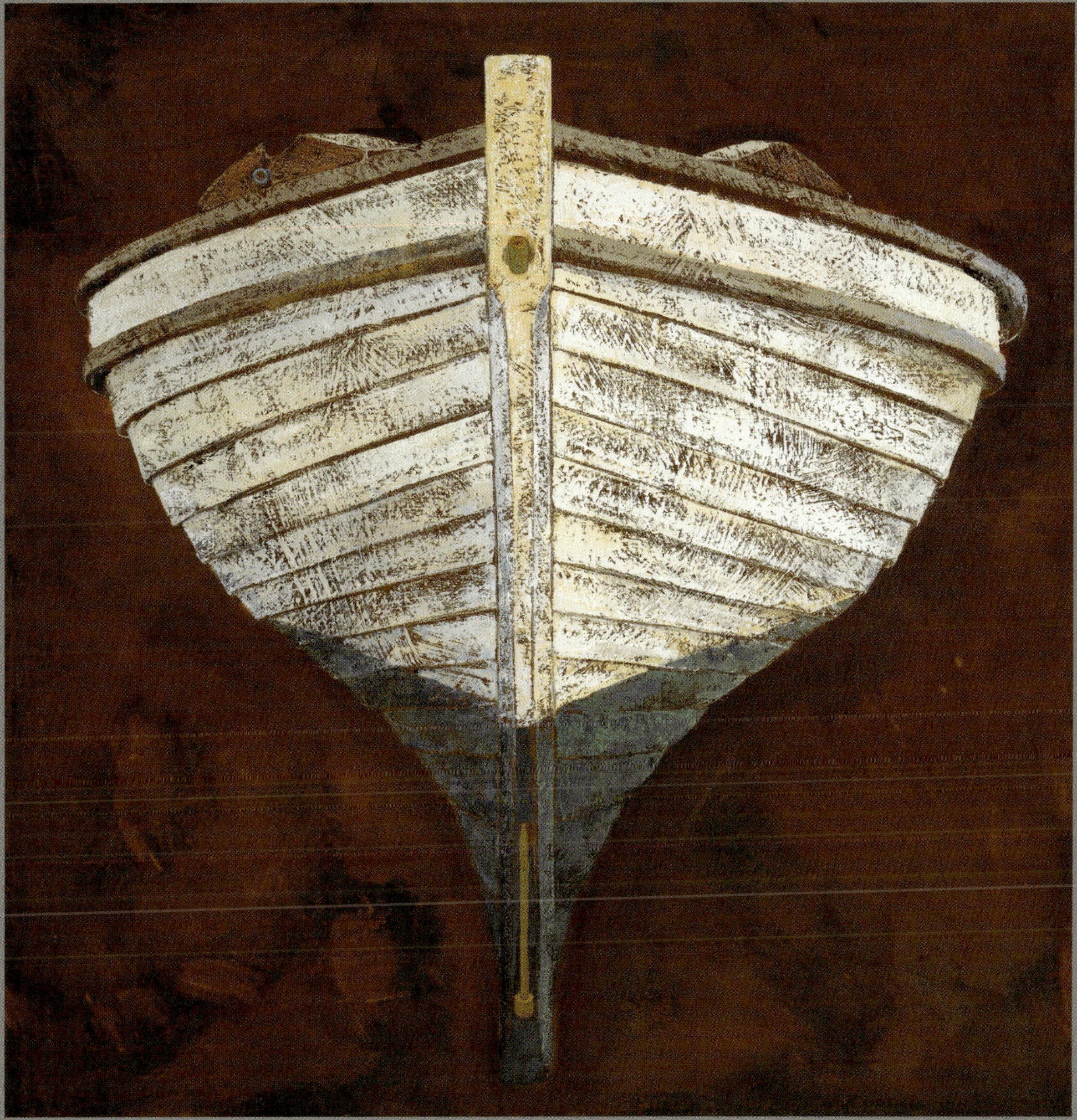

Pilchard Driver
(Oil on linen. 2018. 130 x 90cm)

Mount's Bay Pilchard Driver built by Marcus Pomeroy-Rowden in 2003, from the drawings of the 1902 *Veracity* PZ.111 in Edgar J March's 'Sailing Drifters'. Marcus later went on to build the *Grayhound,* a replica 18th Century three-masted Customs Lugger. The designer of the *Grayhound,* Chris Rees, built the *Spirit of Mystery* based on another Mount's Bay Lugger which was sailed to Australia by Pete Goss. The *Veracity* is now owned by Holly Latham. Thank you to Holly for sending me photos.

(instagram: @lathamstraditionalboatworks)
(Mount's Bay Lugger Association: mbla.co.uk)

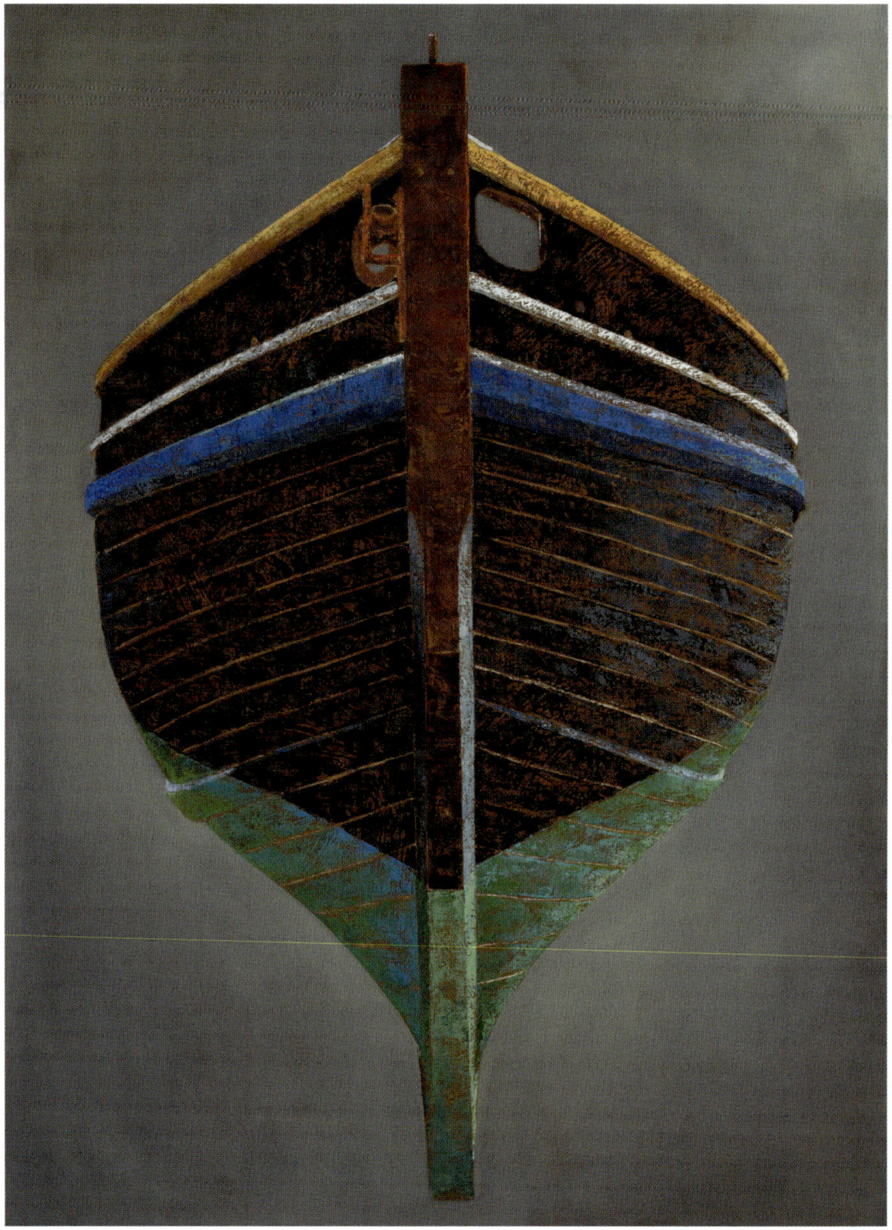

Pilchard Driver
(Oil on linen. 2018. 100 x 90cm)

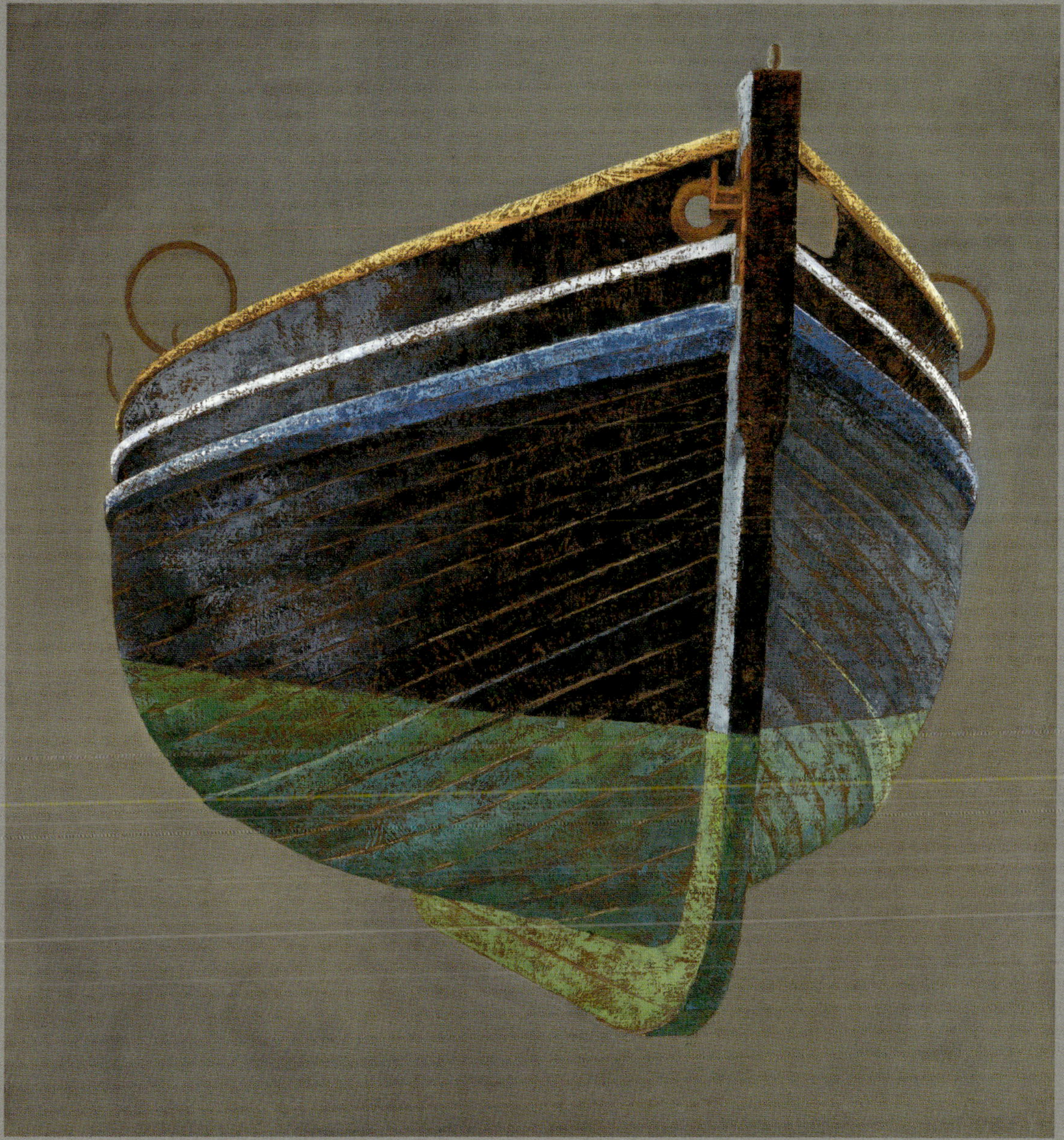

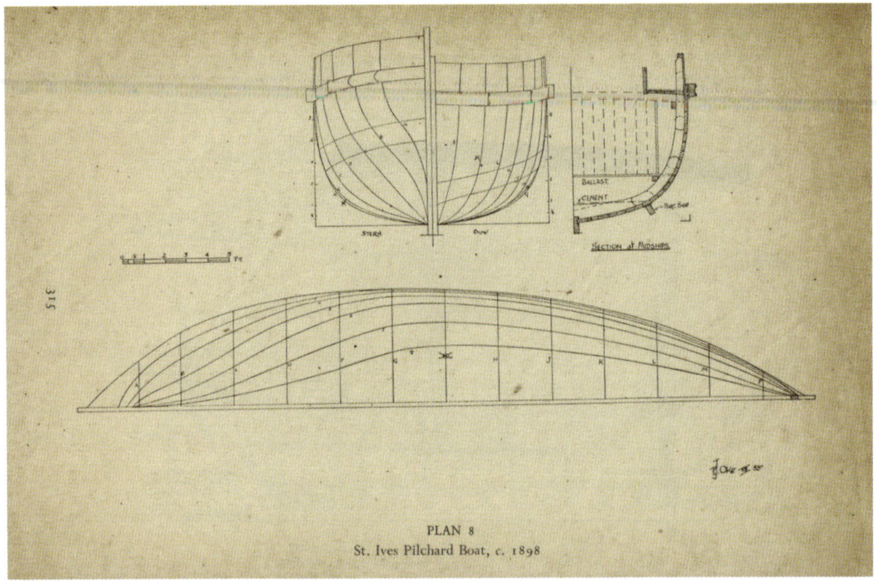

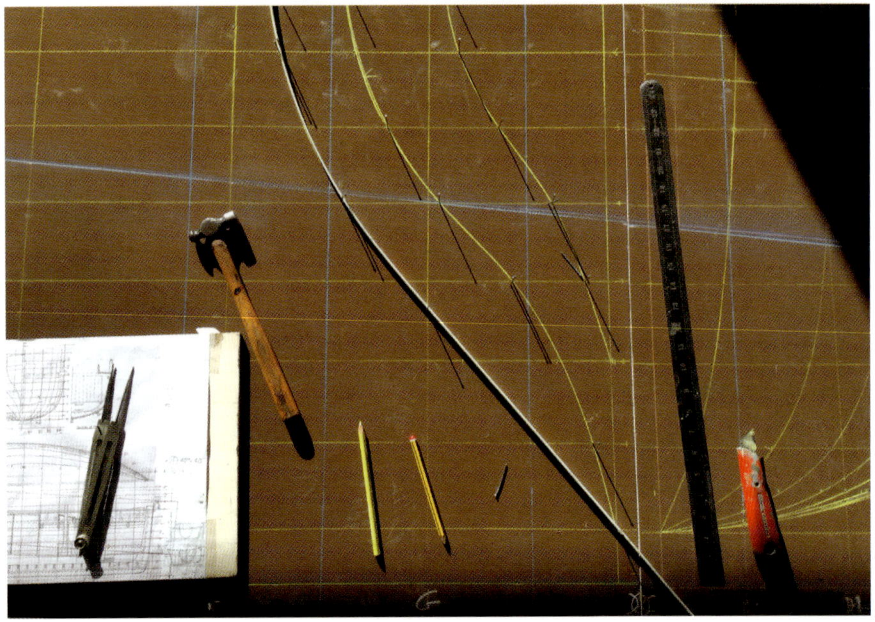

(painting on next page)

St. Ives Pilchard Driver
(Oil on 4 gesso panels. 2019. 122 x 406cm)

There is a lot of room for error scaling up from a line drawing reproduced in a book. But it is thanks to people like Edgar J March and Philip Jesse Oke that the spirit of the vernacular working boat has been preserved.

The painting of the double-ender is the *Godrevy* from St. Ives, built in Porthleven 1898, measured up by Oke in 1935, and the plans are in March's book of *Sailing Drifters*. I have adjusted the line drawings as any boatbuilder would do when scaling up a drawing onto the mould loft floor. I hope I have done justice to the spirit of the boat and the men who build them by eye and rule of thumb.

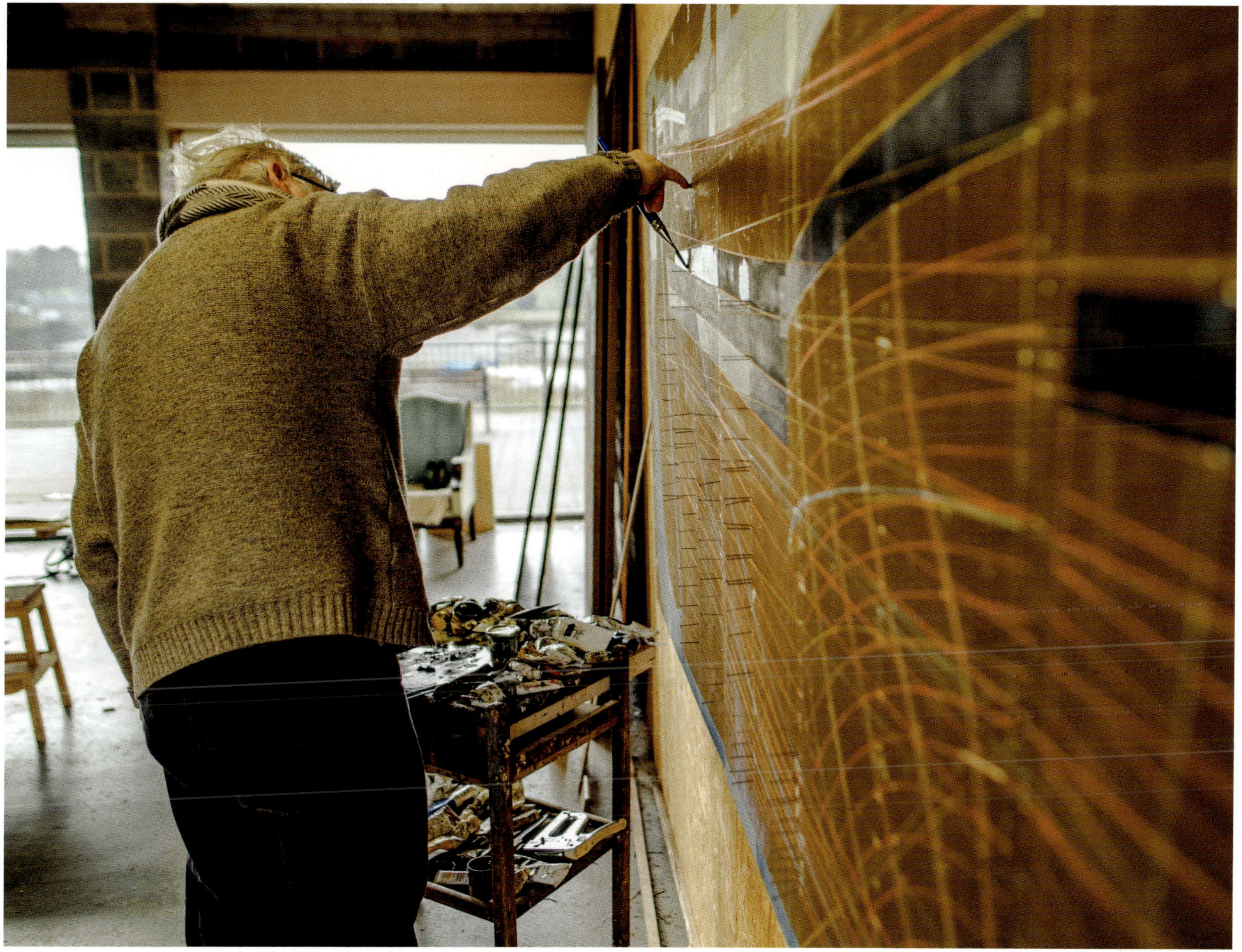

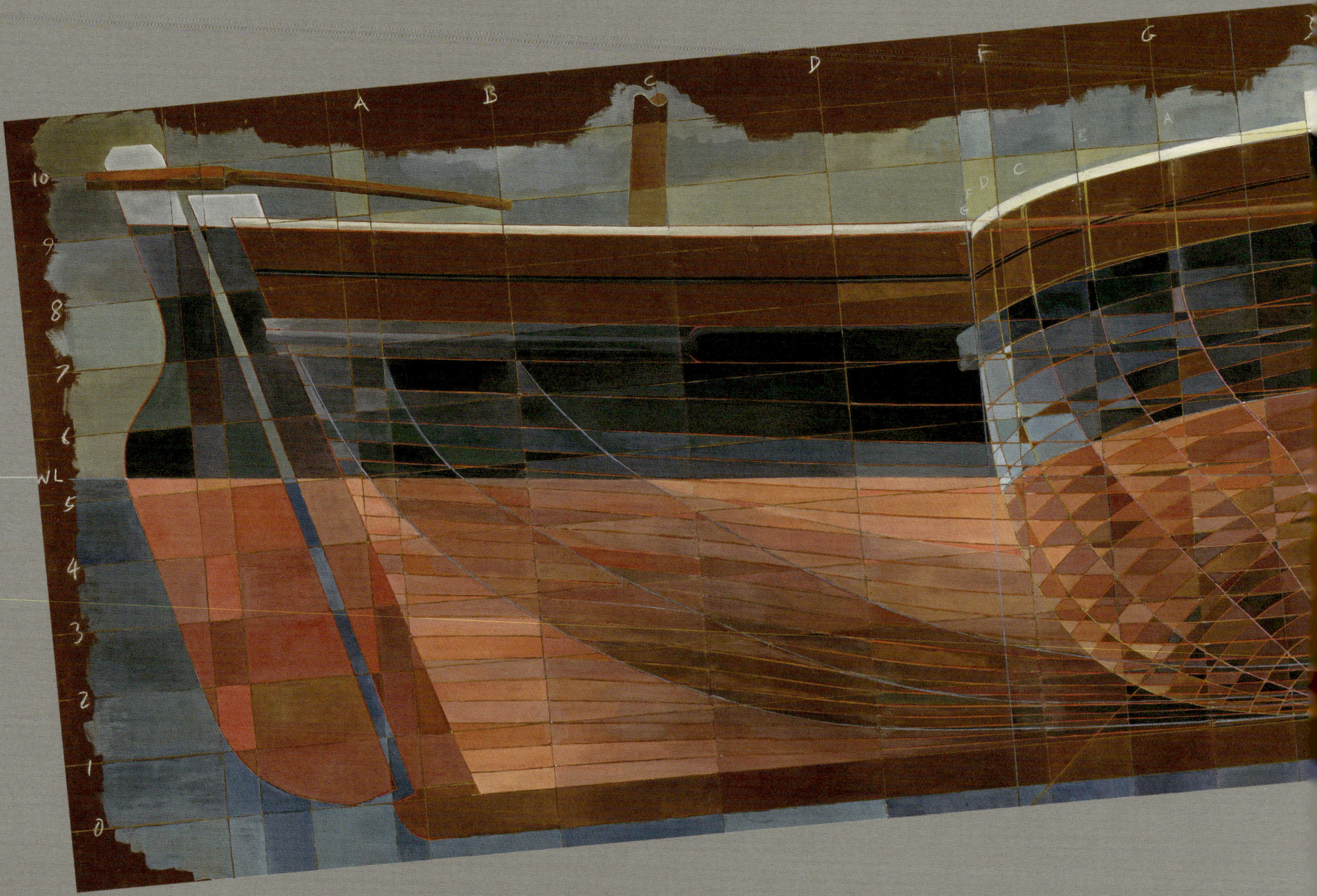
A
B
C
D
F
G
10
9
8
7
6
WL
5
4
3
2
1
0

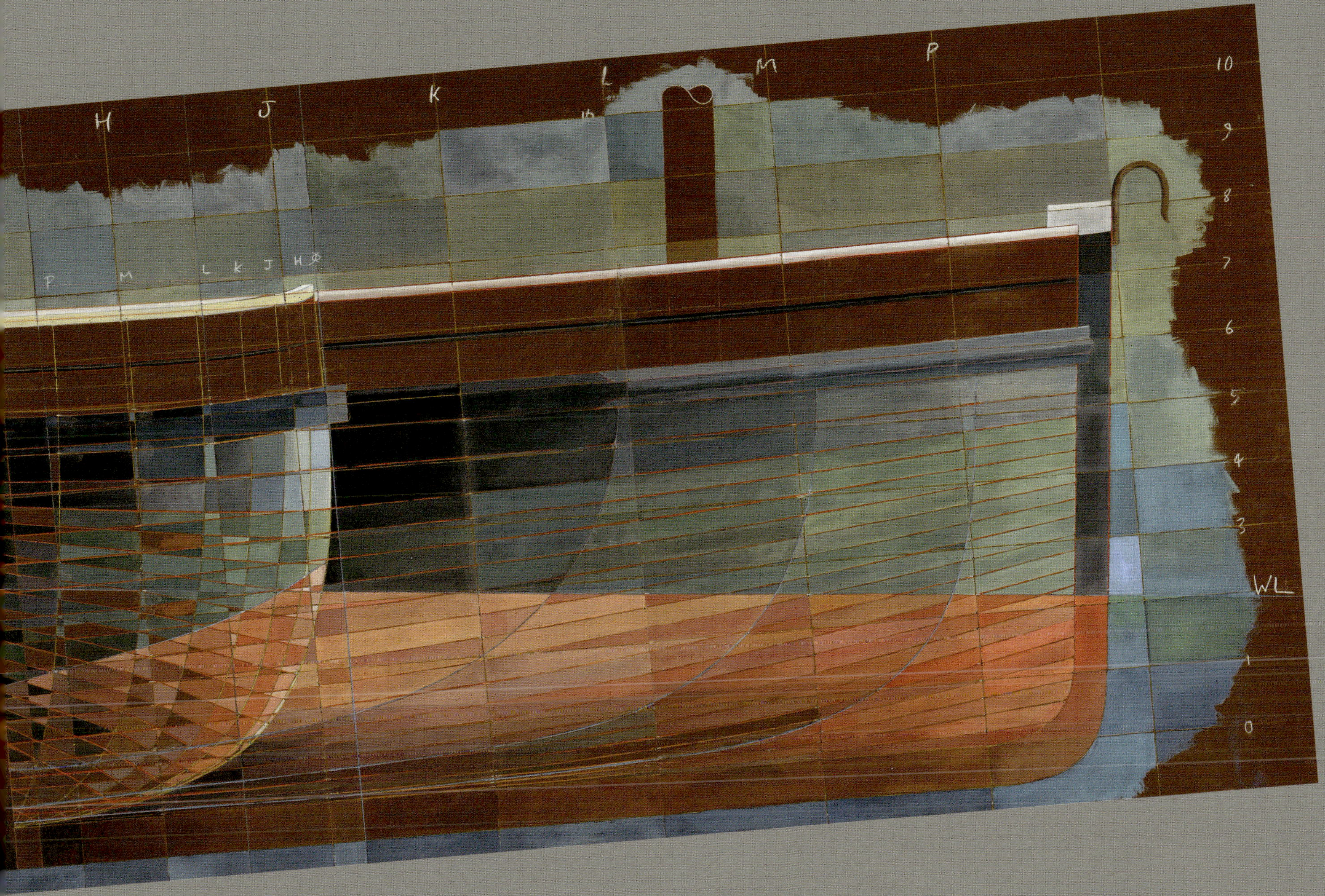
H
J
K
L
M
P
10
9
8
7
6
5
4
3
WL
1
0
P
M
L K J H

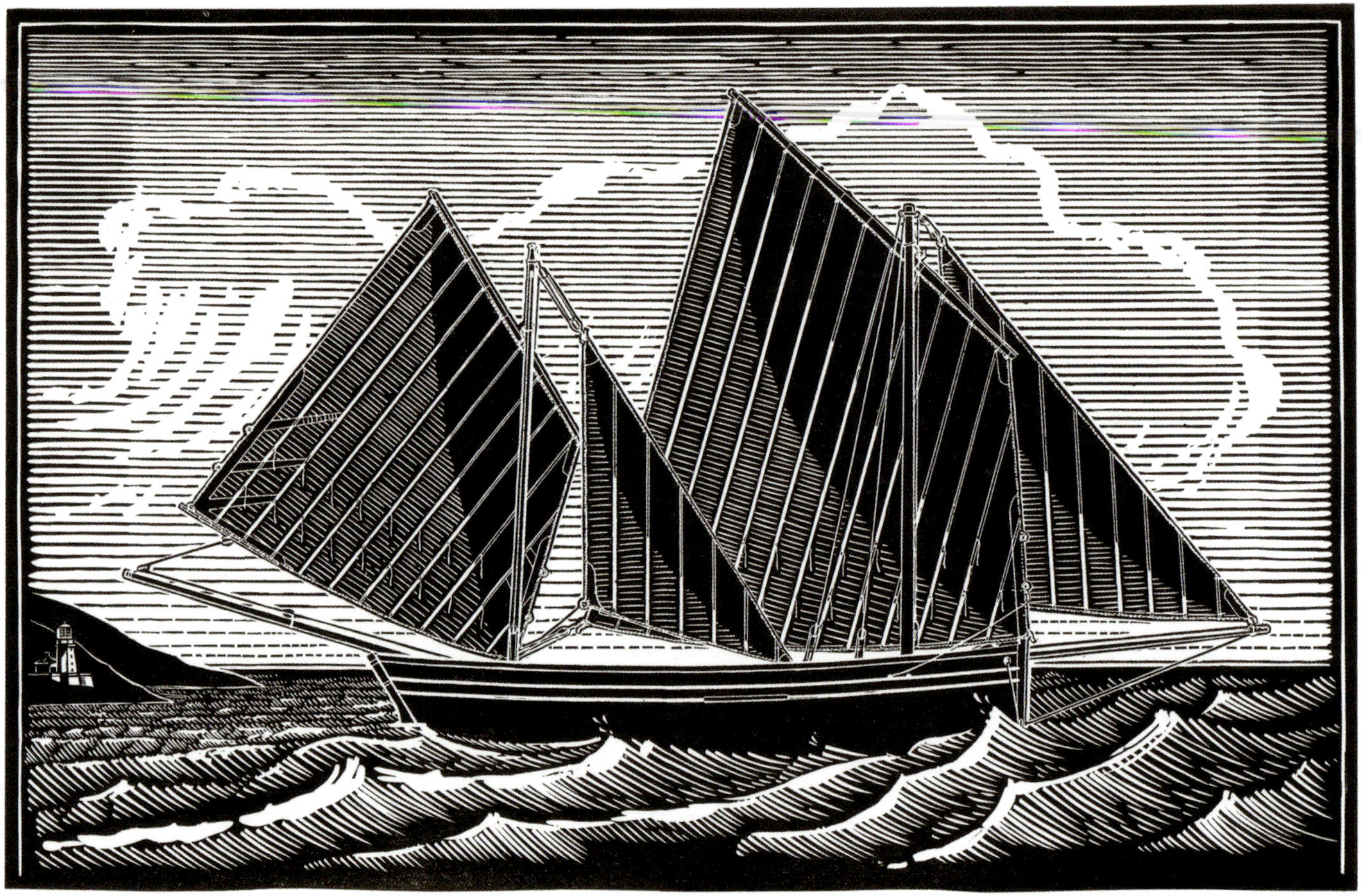

Mevagissey Lugger *(East Cornish Lugger)*
(Linocut. 2019. 36.5 x 56cm)

Edgar March defines the difference between East and West Cornish luggers: 'The Cornish luggers were of two distinct types, instantly recognisable on account of the shape of their sterns. Boats from the East Cornish Ports... invariably had transom sterns, while those west of the Lizard... were generally pointed sterned' or double-enders. However, there are plenty of exceptions to this classification.

Stern of a double-ender
(Oil on linen. 2018. 110 x 120cm)

This is painted from the *Baden Powell* of Kings Lynn, a Wash cockler rebuilt in 2016 at the same yard as the *Bluebell*. She is very similar in size to the *Godrevy* (previous page), and the *Barnabas* which was rebuilt in Cornwall 2008 by the Cornish Maritime Trust and frequently sails from Penzance. The shape of sterns of these double-enders gives these boats their beauty and also their speed through the water. (cornishmaritimetrust.org)

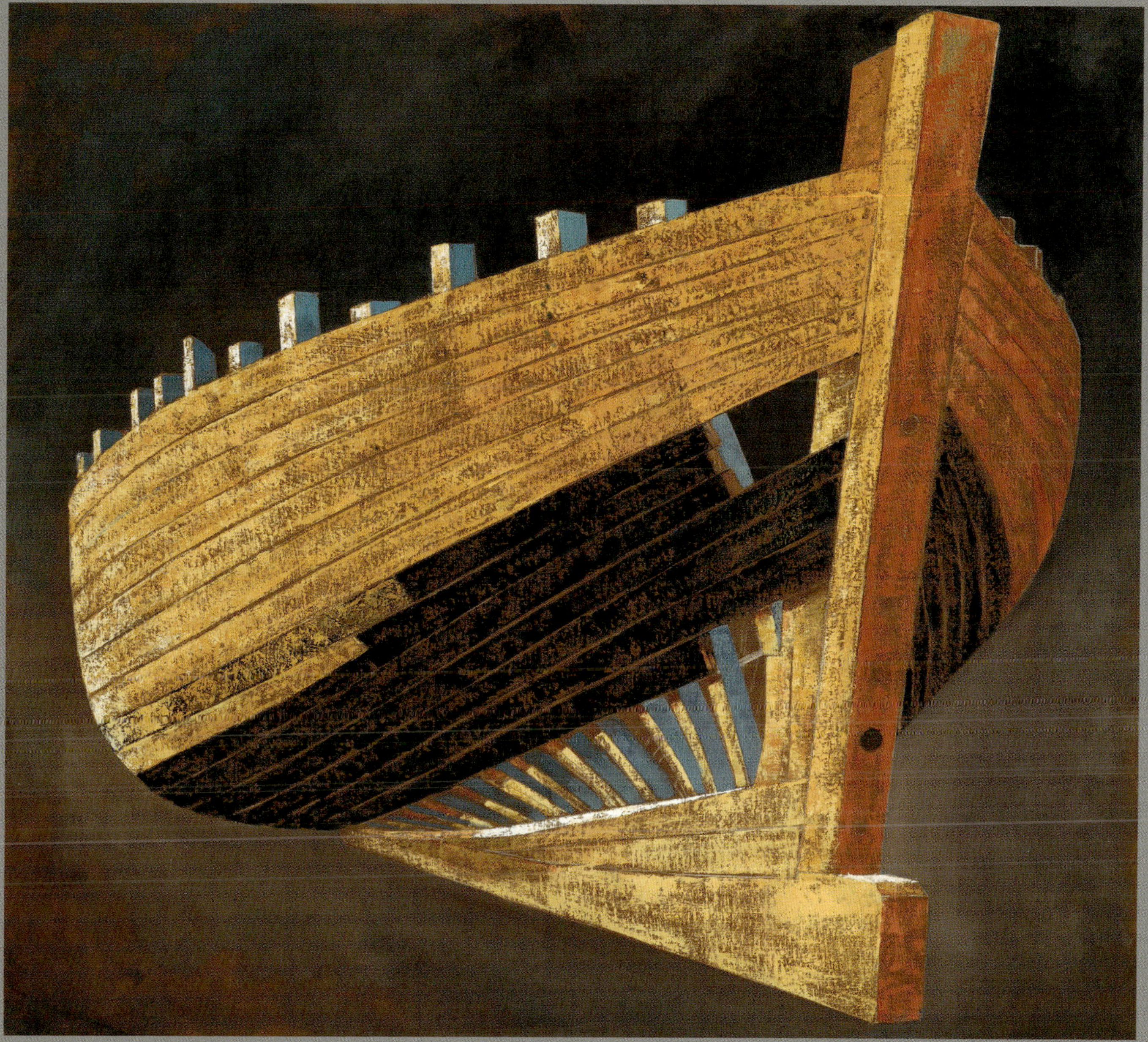

FALMOUTH

Custom House Quay or Town Quay

The small enclosed harbour known as Custom House Quay, or Town Quay, and the adjoining streets and buildings formed the centre of the legal trade and maritime business of the port. However, while the Custom House 'Port of Falmouth,' was created in 1676, there was no single 'Falmouth Harbour'authority until 1870. To this day this little harbour continues to serve as a centre of maritime activity, with moorings for small craft. Despite its tarmacked surface, modern shelters and railings, the large sections of vertically aligned stone walls confirm the antiquity of its basic structure.

Greenbank Quay

Greenbank Quay was one of the principal points of embarkation within the harbour, for passengers travelling overseas by the Falmouth Packets – 1689-1851. The adjoining Greenbank Hotel – a long established hostelry – catered for the comforts of diplomats and other wealthy passengers awaiting their day of departure. A departure into the unknown for many a sole, which all too frequently depended on the state of the wind and weather, rather than any published sailing day.

The quay also gave shelter to humble watermen's boats, open rowing boats which plied to and from Flushing on the other side of the creek.

Flushing

Was a small creek-side hamlet heavily promoted by the Trefusis family in the early 1700s, in an attempt to become the hub of the Post Office packet service. In this bid the quay and wharves were extended, and a good piped supply of fresh water brought to the base of the quay, but to no avail. However, while this bid failed, many of the packet commanders, and their crews, chose Flushing as their home residence, leading to a number of fine houses dating from the mid 1700s.

(At one time, Admiral Edward Pellew lived in Flushing).

Market Strand

Market Strand started off as a beach market, where river traders could land their boat-loads of fruit and vegetables, and other provisions. In time a short quay gave shelter to the landing place, and in the early 1900s, was further extended by the Prince of Wales Pier, which served as a terminal for the river and coastal excursion steamers – a role which is maintained by today's first-class motor launches and their able crews.

Fish Strand

Fish Strand was another beach market, where fresh fish were sold daily. It was here that Lieutenant John Richards Lapenotiere landed from the H.M. schooner Pickle on the morning of November 4th 1805, with the news of the Battle of Trafalgar, and the death of Lord Nelson which he carried to London by horse drawn 'Chaise,' reaching the Admiralty shortly after mid-night on November 6th.

In time riverside quays or wharves were built on the site, and in the mid 1800s the adjoining Gas Works Quay was created, both of which have since been converted into town centre car parking.

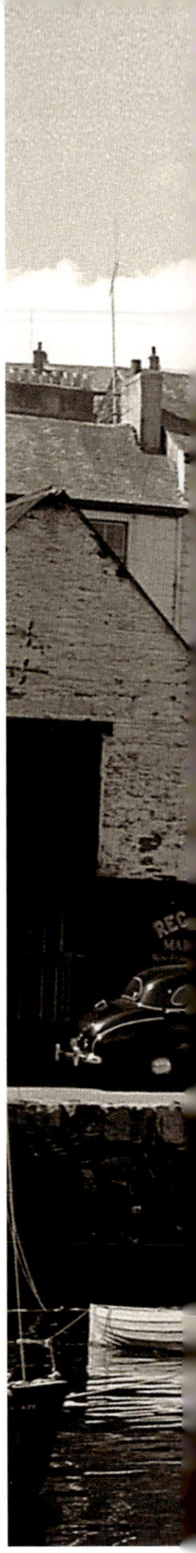

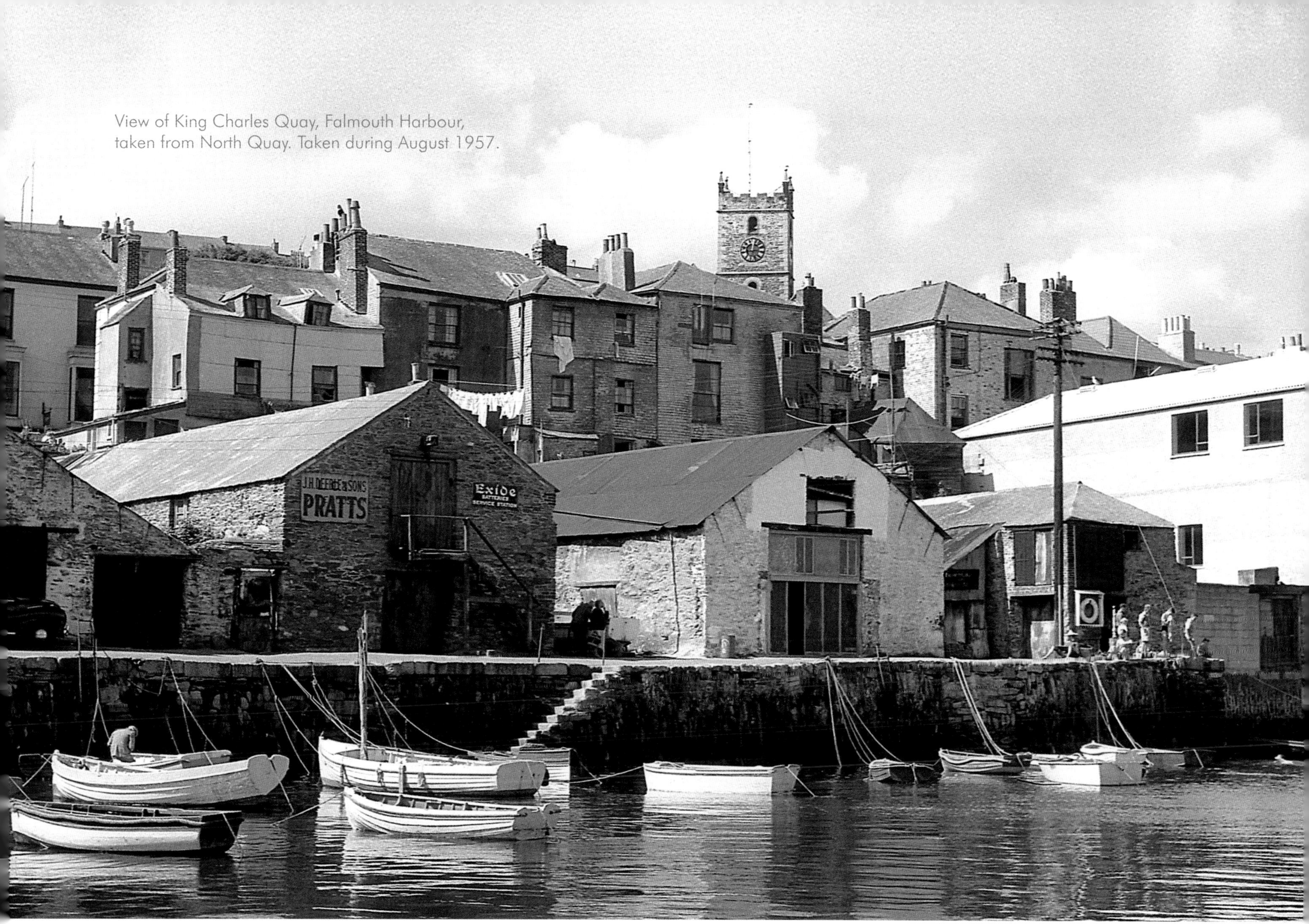

View of King Charles Quay, Falmouth Harbour,
taken from North Quay. Taken during August 1957.

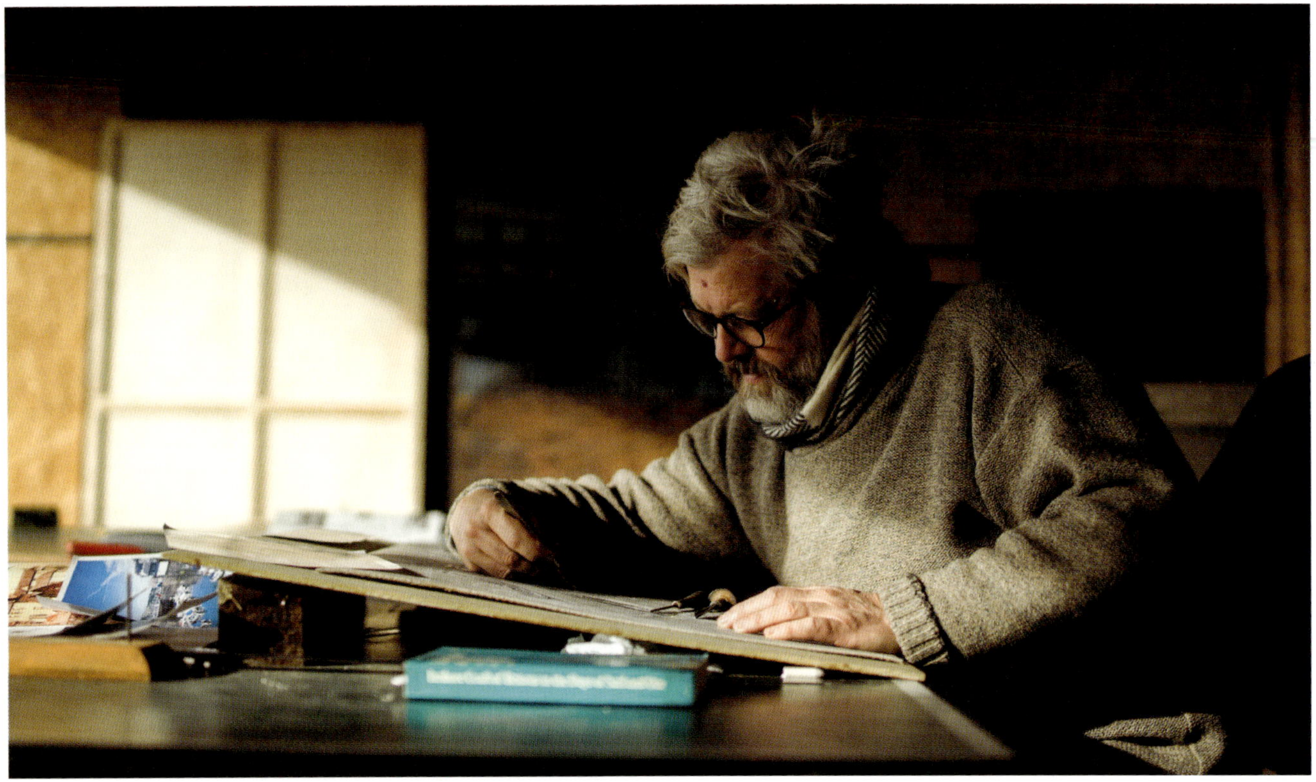

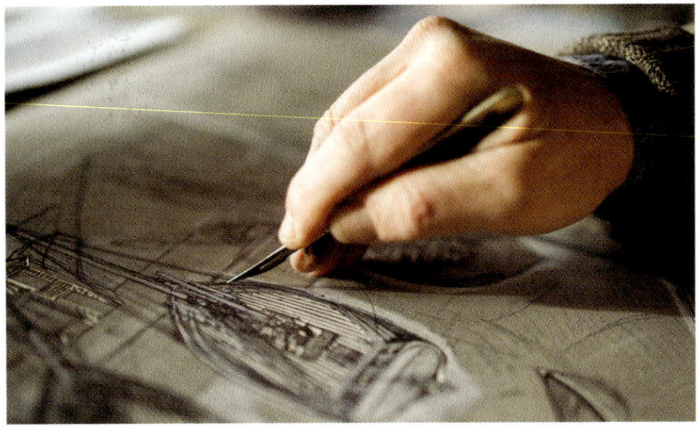

Falmouth Town Quay
(Linocut. 2019. 52 x 70cm)

Now known as Custom House Quay. This linocut shows an imagined scene of the harbour filled with traditional boats: the fruit schooner *Rhoda Mary,* the *Pellew,* four small pilchard drivers, in the foreground the St. Ives double-ender, the steam tug *St. Denys* against the outer wall of the harbour and the *Grayhound* in full sail (grayhoundluggersailing.co.uk).

Coincidently many of Falmouth's fast fruit schooners where built by Thomas Harvey, a shipbuilder from my home town in his Ipswich shipyard. But one of the fastest, the *Rhoda Mary*, was built in 1868 at Point, near Falmouth in a shipyard owned by John Stephens of Devoran.

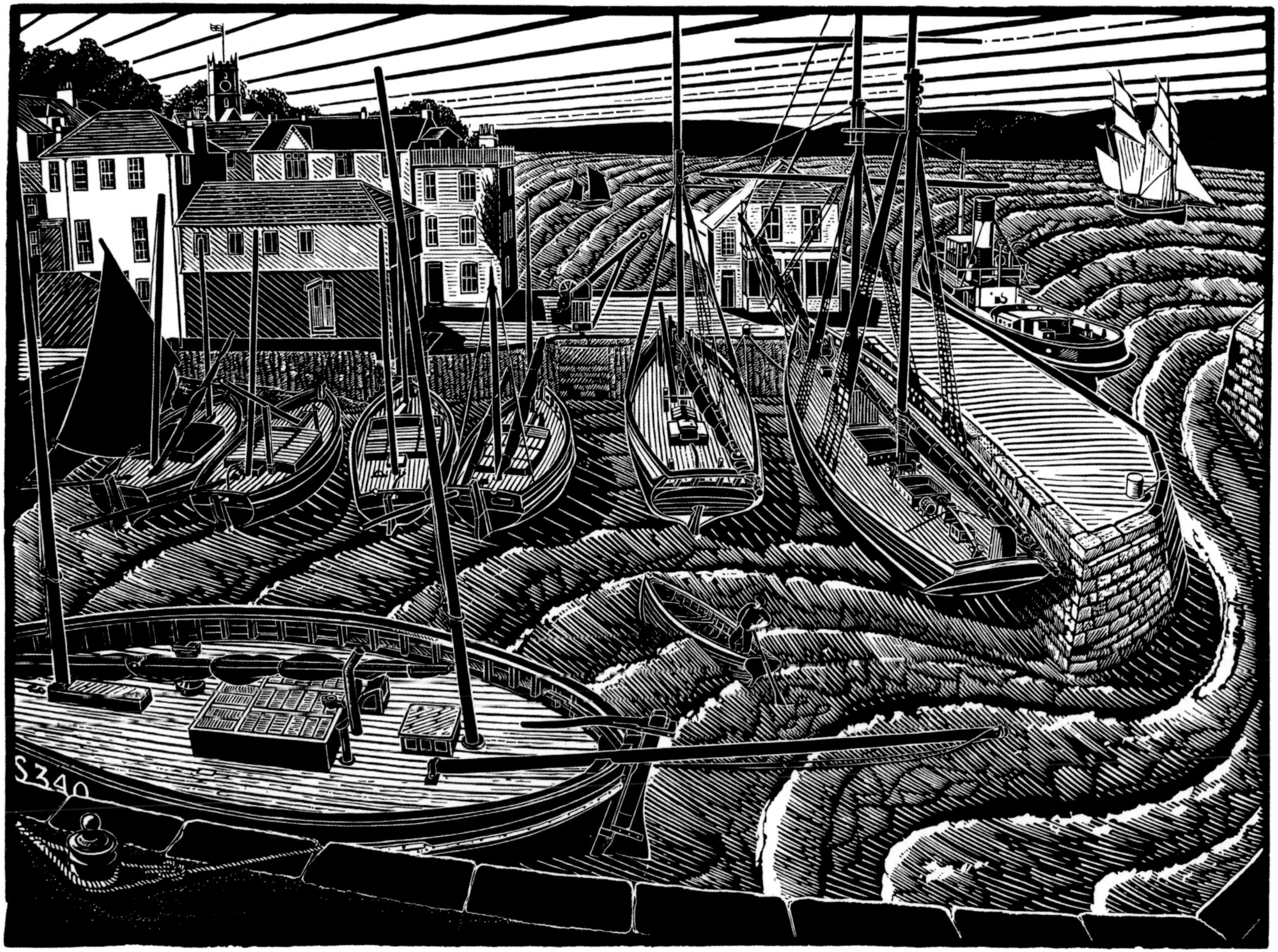
S340

James Dodds was born in the east coast fishing town of Brightlingsea, and trained as a shipwright in Maldon. He then studied painting at Chelsea College of Art and the Royal College of Art, London. He is also a printmaker and has conceived, illustrated and hand-produced a series of artists books under the imprint of Jardine Press.

Selected Solo Exhibitions

1983: 'Icarus', **Minories**, Colchester
1984, '95, '98, 2000: **Aldeburgh Festival**
1985: 'Ship of Fools', **Hatton Gallery**, Newcastle upon Tyne
1986: 'Fish, Flesh or Fowl', **Christchurch Mansion**, Ipswich
1989, '90, '95, '97: **Printworks**, Colchester
1989, '92, '95, '99, '09, '14, '18: **Bircham Contemporary Arts**, Norfolk
1990, '94, '05: **Chapel Galleries**, Essex
1992: **Sue Rankin Gallery**, London (2-man show with John Bratby RA)
2001: **North House Gallery**, Manningtree, (with John Reay)
2001, '07: **Art Exchange**, Essex University Gallery

2001: 'Shipshape', **Firstsite at The Minories**, Colchester
'Shipshape' tour:
2002: **Whitstable & Hearne Bay Museums & Art Galleries**, Kent
Black Swan Arts, Frome, Somerset
Quay Arts, Newport, Isle of Wight
Bowes Museum, Barnard Castle, Co. Durham
2003: **National Maritime Museum Cornwall**, Falmouth
2004: **National Maritime Museum**, Greenwich
2005: **Time & Tide**, Great Yarmouth
Buckenham Gallery, Southwold
Hartlepool Art Gallery, Hartlepool
Highland Council, Thurso & Wick, Scotland
Fermoy Gallery, King's Lynn Arts Centre, King's Lynn

2004, '06, '07, '09, '11, '13, '15, '16, '17, '18: **Messum's**, London
2005, '08, '12, '16: **Hayletts Gallery**, Maldon
2008: **Salthouse 08**: Norfolk (mixed show)
2010, '12, '17: **Dowling Walsh Gallery**, Rockland, Maine. USA
2013: 'Masterpieces, Art & East Anglia' **Sainsbury Centre**, (mixed show)
2015: 'Wood to Water' **Firstsite**, Colchester

YouTube films:

Beneath The Surface
Victoria Matthews. 2002

Artist at Work
Mary Dodds. 2013

Shaped by the Sea
Emily Harris. 2014

Timepeace
Timelapse film painting a Colchester Fishing Smack. 2015

Gipsy
Timelapse film painting a Yarmouth Drifter. 2017

Pellew
Timelapse film painting a Pilot Cutter. 2018

Falmouth Quay Punt
Timelapse film painting a Falmouth Quay Punt. 2018

Jardine Press Books

Peter Grimes, *George Crabbe 1984*
Wild Man of Orford, *Allan Drummond 1995*
Wild Man of Wivenhoe, *Martin Newell 1997*
Alphabet of Boats, *James Dodds 1998*
Black Shuck, *Martin Newell 1999*
ABC of Boat Bits, *James Dodds 2000*
A-Z of Printmaking, *Elly Robinson 2000*
Knock John Ship, *James Dodds 2001*
The Song of the Waterlily, *Martin Newell 2003*
Longshore Drift, *Katrina Porteous 2005*
Blue Lonnen, *Katrina Porteous 2007*
River Colne Shipbuilders, *John Collins & James Dodds 2009*
Tide Lines, *Ian Collins 2011*
Wood to Water, *catalogue James Dodds at firstsite 2015*
The Green Children, *Martin Newell 2015*
Tracks in the Sand, *2017*

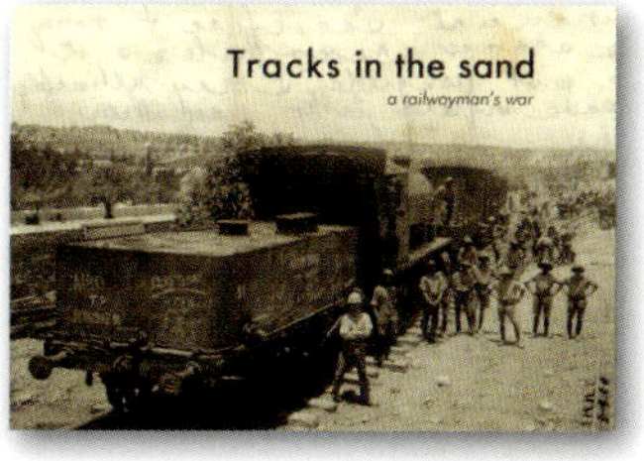

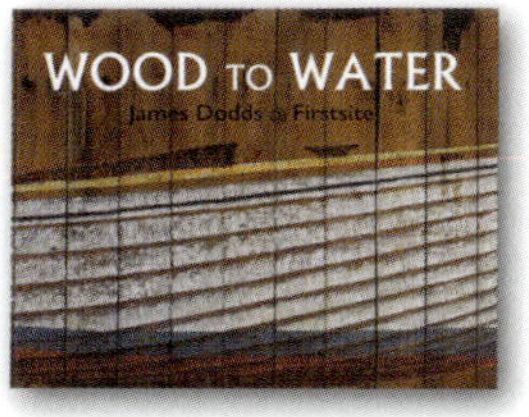

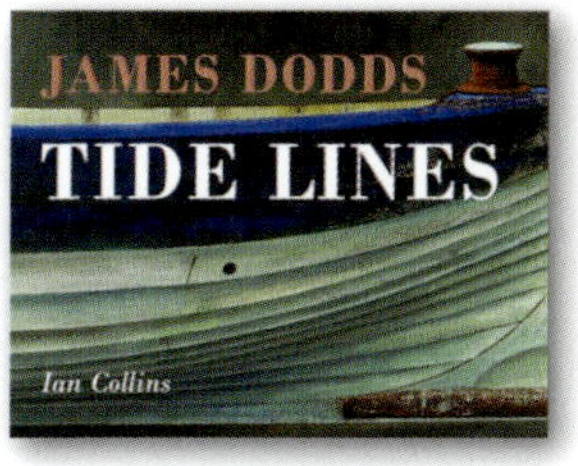

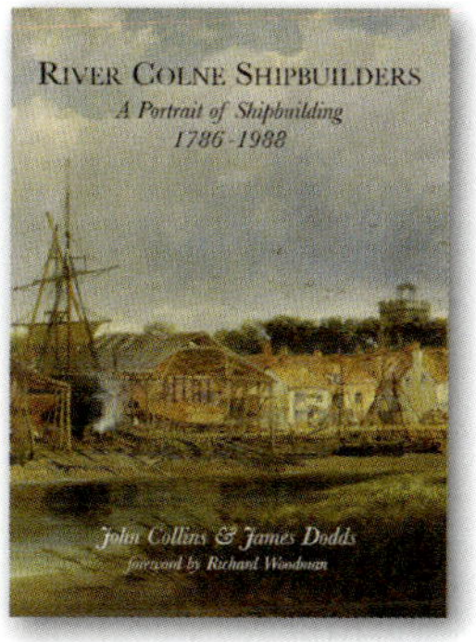

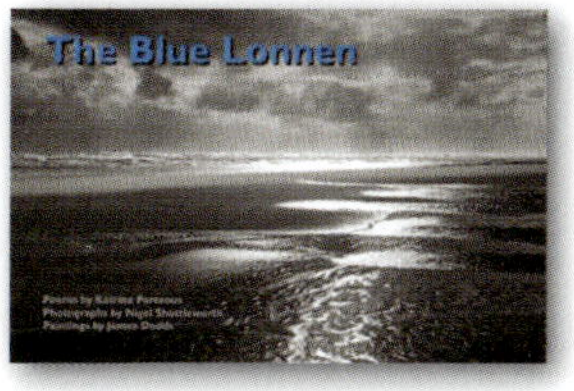

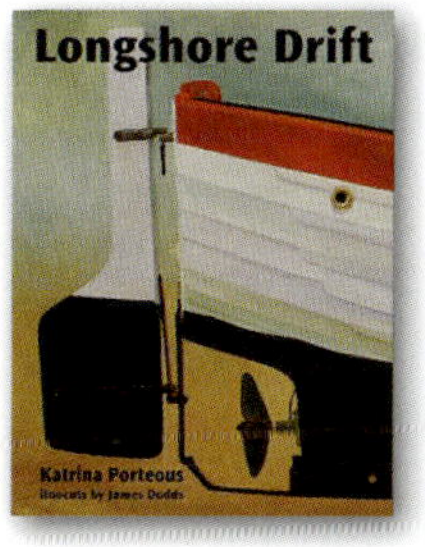

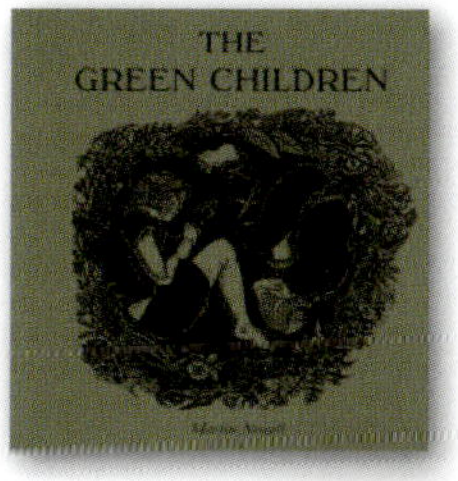

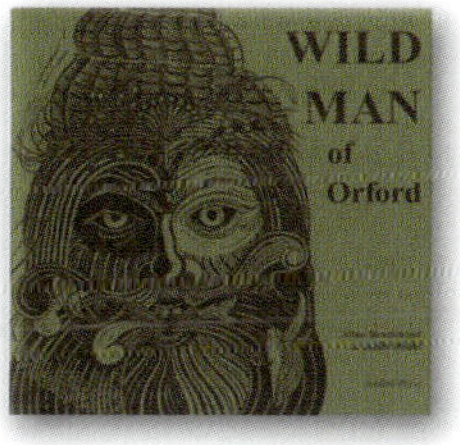

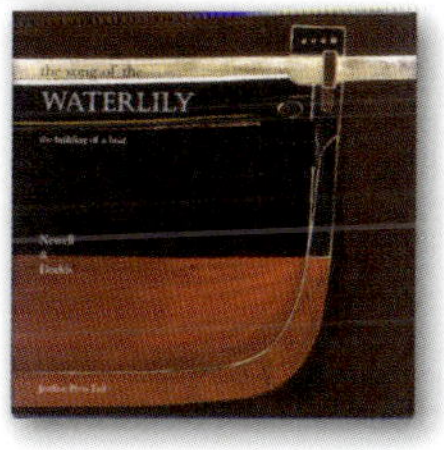

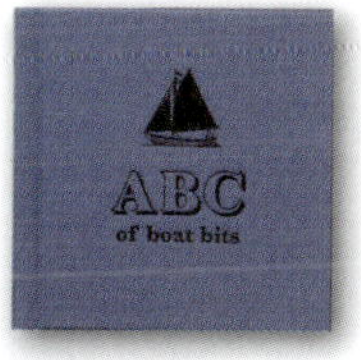

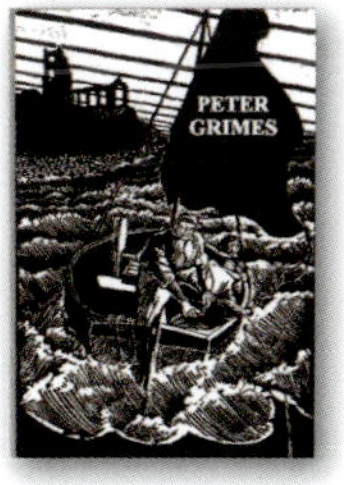

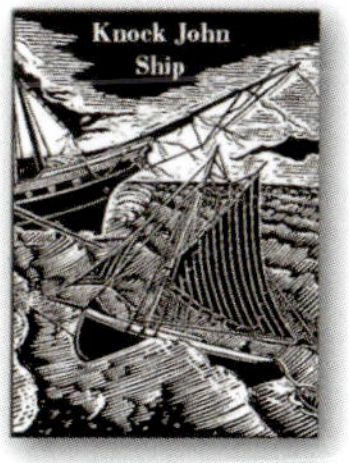

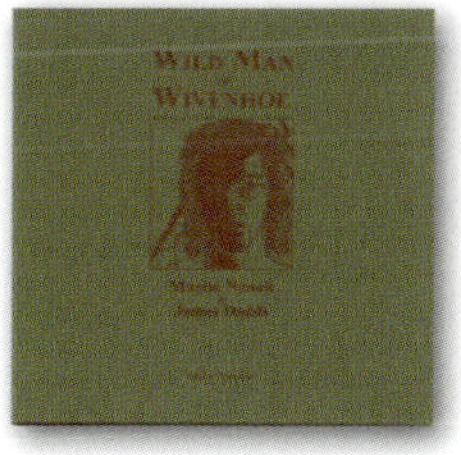

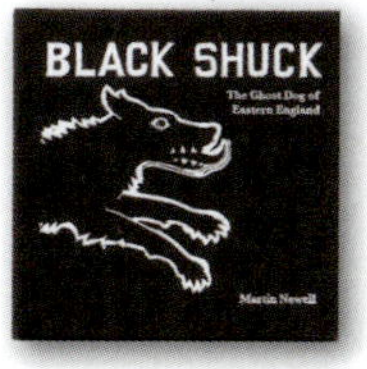

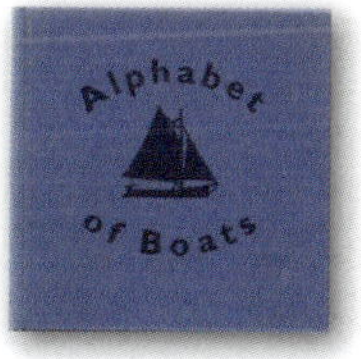

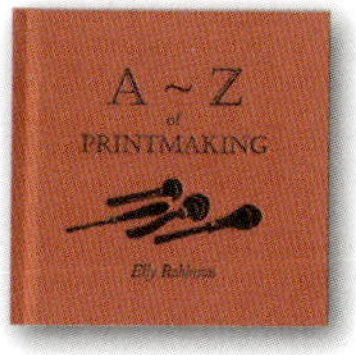

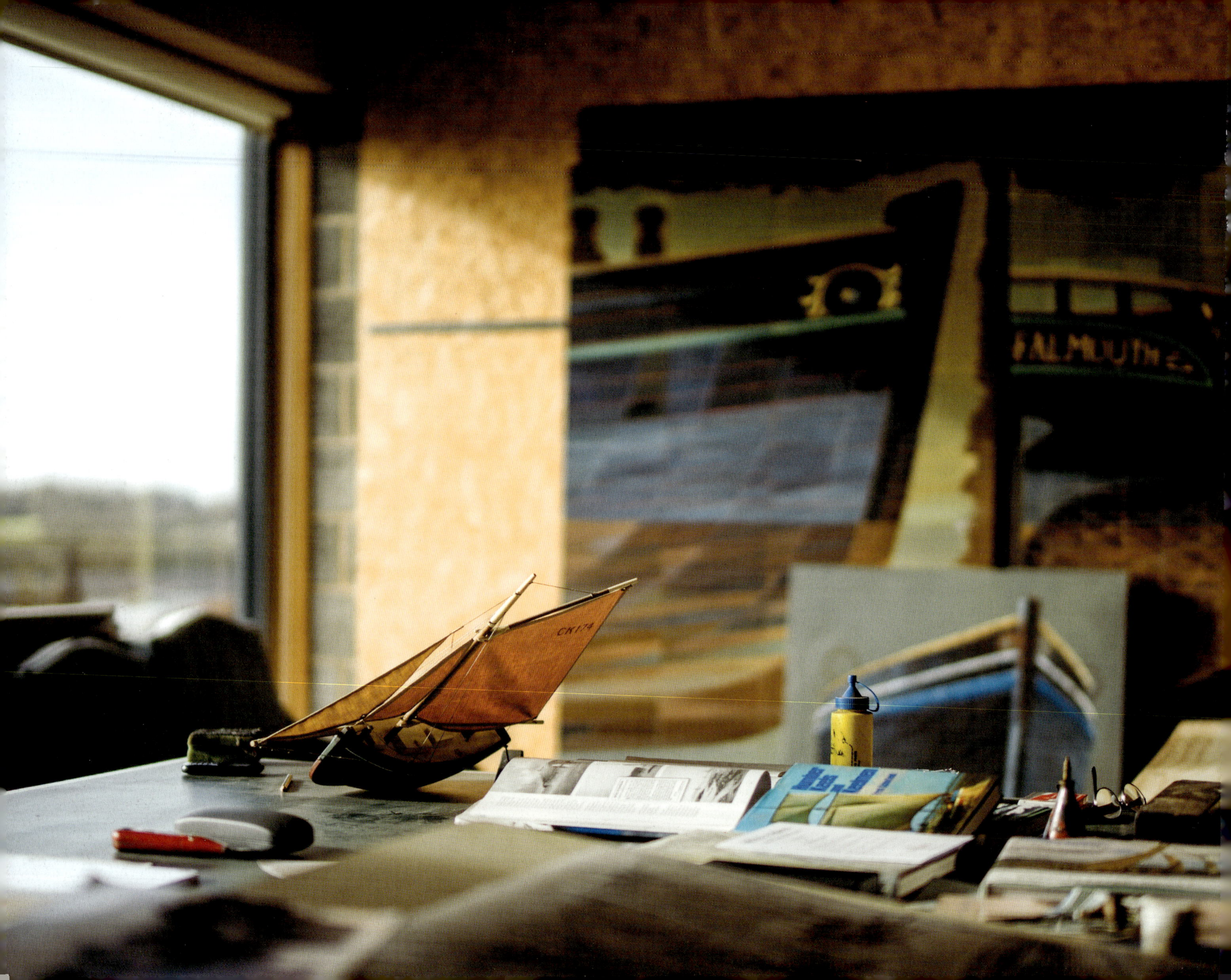
CK174
FALMOUTH